MY
SPACE
ODYSSEY

MY
SPACE
ODYSSEY

BILL BELL

XULON PRESS

Xulon Press
2301 Lucien Way #415
Maitland, FL 32751
407.339.4217
www.xulonpress.com

Paperback ISBN-13: 978-1-6628-5759-1
Dust Jacket ISBN-13: 978-1-6628-5760-7
Ebook ISBN-13: 978-1-6628-5761-4

FOREWORD

Mr. Bill Bell has been a great asset to Lockheed EMSCO in supporting **NASA** at the Johnson Space Center. I have known Bill as a Safety and Mission Assurance Engineer and a good friend for over 25 years. I am happy to recommend this book to all of the young and old who love an excellent Space Journey. Bill has truly lived his dream for his Space and Faith Journey. I know that this book will inspire you to live out your dreams also. Bill has always exhibited superior work habits and with high technical competence, for the Engineering and Safety requirements for Shuttle Payloads, and for the Spacewalkers. Repeatedly, He has been involved in demanding tasks with short due dates. Bill was a key member of the Shuttle 51A Satellite recovery mission on November 8, 1984—-this mission was an historical Event. Bill furnished valuable engineering support for the US Air Force and NASA Ozone Balloon Flight experiments.

Recently I had the privilege of working with Bill as his Project manager at Lockheed Aircraft Services in California for the Air Force Department of Defense for the Pacer Coin Project. This project required a top secret clearance. Bill was involved with Systems Engineering tasks that were demanding. Bill was there to form working teams within the Department of Defense (DOD) US Air force and Lockheed Aircraft Services for The Pacer Coin Project. Bill as a project leader and working with the teams developed valuable input as well as developing communication lines between the Air Force Department of Defense and Lockheed Aircraft Services.

Bill Bell's contribution in leading numerous teams in operational safety and design concepts has been instrumental, in his NASA counterparts arriving at logical Engineering decisions.

Rey Rivas
Project Manager
Lockheed EMSCO

ACKNOWLEDGMENT

This book is dedicated to my Father, Mother, Sisters, and my Grandparents, for each one's Love, integrity, and Faith has left an impression on my life. By following my Faith Compass on my Space and Faith Journey.

To my dear wife, Susan, and best friend, who encouraged me to write the story of my Space Odyssey.

To my children, Julie, Bryan, Craig, and Christopher, my precious treasures. May they experience their own Journey.

To Emily Osburn of The Woodlands Writing Group, and to each of the members who helped me finish writing my book.

To all of my faithful Mentors in life, who believed in me, and to all my Friends who made my Journey a dream come true.

I want to dedicate this book to each of you. May we all be blessed by the grace of our **Lord.**

MY SPACE ODYSSEY

From a dream to reality, my Space Odyssey began long ago. This book is about the voyage marked by the success and tragedy of the Space Program. It is the story of my life, an Autobiography of the experiences growing up in a small Texas Community, thru high school, military, and college. I following my dream of one day supporting the **NASA** Space Program. And through all of my Journeys in Space and Faith, especially my Faith. I want my faith to inspire you to take your own journey in life.

I followed my dream; by supporting **NASA** In the field of Safety and Mission Assurance (S&MA). It has allowed me to support the Space Shuttle Payloads and the Astronauts for their Spacewalks. Before that I was assigned to a number of Apollo Moon Missions and the Saturn V Rocket Program. I was blessed with Caring Parents and Faithful Mentors, who helped me believe in my dream, as they enabled me to dream even bigger, on my Space and Faith Journey.

President John F. Kennedy in 1961 made his World Famous Speech to the American Public. This speech was about a challenge to the people of the United States to dream big about putting a man on the moon and returning him safely back to earth. It was a challenge for each of us to look upward and dream. But even more, it was a challenge to show the world the commitment and capabilities of a United American People. The Space race had begun. So on July 20, 1969 we put the first humans on the moon, Apollo

11, "The Eagle has landed." With Mission Commander Neil Armstrong and pilot Buzz Aldrin landed the Lunar Module. American's Space program did not stop with Apollo; no the Moon was never the end goal. The Moon was only the beginning and reaching the Moon was just the first step in opening the universe to human exploration into Space. The Space Shuttle has placed many satellites in space bringing communications and education to every corner of our world. Also, the Shuttle has placed Observatories in space, letting us look into the Universe by using the Hubble Space Telescope. **NASA** has worked in harmony with Other Nations to build the International Space Station (ISS). There has been success and failures along the way. We are at the end of the Shuttle Program, with its retirement in 2011. **NASA** Needs a clear goal for further exploration into space. We as a Nation call on **NASA** to lead us once again to dream.

I served in the Army during the Vietnam War. I was assigned to the Army Security Agency at Fort Devens, Massachusetts and retained a Top Secret Classification. Here I learned how to Discyper Secret Code. It has enabled me to work with **NASA** and the Department of Defense (DOD) for the Space Shuttle Missions and the Pacer Coin Project for the Air force.

I was first assigned to work at the **NASA** site in New Orleans for the Saturn V Rocket Program. Here **NASA** built the World's largest rocket to transport the Apollo Capsule into space.

Later I was assigned to work at the Shuttle Avionics Integration Laboratory (SAIL) at **NASA**, Johnson Space Center. The SAIL supported the entire Space Shuttle Program to perform integrated verification tests. The Laboratory was utilized by the Astronauts to train for their up- coming Missions. My responsibility was to ensure the safety of each astronaut. The Laboratory also contained Firing Room Launch Equipment identical to that used at the Kennedy Space Center, where complete ground verification as well as countdown and abort operations could be tested and simulated. At this Laboratory, My Manager was Christopher C. Kraft, who in the past was Director of Flight Operations in Mission Control at **NASA.**

We were a unified group of employees, **NASA** and Contractors all working as a team to achieve our space journey. Along my way, I experienced my faith Journey.

Together we worked to build the Space Shuttle and the International Space Station (ISS).

I was an extra in a movie, "SPACE" by James Mitchner, filmed at **NASA**, Johnson Space Center.

Supporting the Space Shuttle Payloads and Spacewalkers, for Safety and Mission Assurance.

Exploring our UNIVERSE with the Hubble Space Telescope.

CHUCK YEAGER, SPUTNIK, AND HIGH SCHOOL

Chuck Yeager has always been someone who I could relate too, for all this man has accomplished by pushing the envelope in avionation. He was born February 13, 1923. Chuck Yeager a former United States Air Force Flight Officer and a fighter pilot during WWII. After the war, Yeager became a test pilot of many types of aircraft, including experimental rocket-powered aircraft. He was the first human to officially break the sound barrier on October 14, 1947. Yeager flew the experimental Bell X-1 at Mach 1 speed at an altitude of 45,000 ft. Yeager later set a new record of Mach 2.44. After his historic flight, he made a perfect landing at Edwards Air force Base. Yeager's triumph was followed by a celebration at Pancho's Fly Inn, a hangout for the Test Pilots, with a free steak dinner and all the beer one could drink. During the Vietnam War, Yeager was promoted to Brigadier General. Yeager was raised on a small ranch like mine. I find inspiration in this noble person, for all he has achieved in life.

Because of my Dad, I was taught to have respect for all military personnel and their families. You see, my Father served in WWII in the Navy. He was assigned duty in the Pacific where he served aboard a Navy Destroyer.. My Dad achieved the rank of Chief Petty Officer. The men on his ship were proud to have served beside my father. He could not speak of the war until many years later; he will always be my Hero. After the war, my Father used his GI Bill to further his education while he served in the Naval Reserve at Corpus Christi Texas. My Father and my Mother were married in Houston, Texas. I was <u>born under a big oak tree</u>; a huge oak tree that was covering my Grandmothers house. My Mother was visiting my Grandmother when she began having labor pains. The family doctor was called and came as quickly as possible. I was born in Ingleside Texas, Just outside of Corpus Christi, Texas.

I was blessed with talents from my **Lord** that brought me to **NASA** as a young Engineer. I was ready to work with all of the talented Astronauts who shared a common dream. I am proud to say that I did my part for the Safety of the Space Shuttle. We were inspired by it, and when tragedy happened, it saddened the world. I was there for it all- from the first Shuttle Mission STS- 1, until the STS-51L Mission and beyond. We have launched a Space Shuttle with a payload of the Hubble Telescope, capable of viewing faraway stars in the Universe put there by our **Lord.**

I want to share my Space Odyssey during my Faith and Space journey, and how I experienced it, by pursing my dream. To help you understand the work that I was responsible for, The Safety and Mission Assurance for the Space Shuttle Payloads and the men who put them into orbit- the Spacewalkers.

I was blessed on my journey, by a loving **God**, who made each day at **NASA** an adventure and a dream come true.

My journey at **NASA** did not come easy. It was hard with all of the failures and setbacks that one had to overcome. I reached my dreams by always believing in my Faith no matter how distance they become. And staying the course with them thru trial and error, and finally success.

You must believe and persevere. "You must look fear in the face and believe in your self' (Eleanor Roosevelt.)

I was given opportunities to advance my self, by having Mentors working one-on-one with me. I cannot tell you enough about having Mentors that believe in you. My journey with Space, Engineering, life, and Faith all began at the same time and place in a small American town of Ingleside, Texas. When the Moon was still unreachable, a young boys dream could take him to the stars. I remember looking at the Moon, and wondering how far away it looked. The Moon was a metaphor for the unattainable: "You might as well ask for the Moon," they used to say.

On October 4, 1957, on this day the Russians launched there Satellite –Sputnik-1. The Space race had officially started with this great achievement in space. We must prove our selves once again to the whole World, we must dream of Space and where it will take our Nation. Sputnik was only a 23-inch diameter polished metal sphere and with 4 external radio antennas, to broadcast radio pulses. It made 1440 completed orbits of the Earth. This success precipitated the American Sputnik crisis and triggered the Space Race, a part of the Cold War. The launch of Sputnik ushered in new political, military, technological, and scientific developments.

My Parents and Grandparents were truly involved in helping me become the person I am today. With their strong guidance in helping me find my place in this world. They insisted that I follow my dream and never stop. As a small community, we were blessed by the fact that Humble Oil and Refining Co had located in our Town. This meant jobs, security, housing development, funds for new schools, infrastructures, and everyone knew that we were the envy of all the surrounding areas. Our city was on the Map. I enjoyed all of the benefits including the new library, with access to new information on Space articles. Humble Oil hired my Father and soon he advanced to be a foreman over 50 men. He worked many hours, and came home late in the evening. Mother always had the evening meal heated and my Sisters and I enjoyed dad's companiship. Our Town offered another benefit, two additional churches. My Parents, Grandparents, me and my two sisters, were always at church early Sunday morning. Later in life I experienced a Faith Journey. As a young boy, I grew up contented in knowing that life was good to me. I had everything that truly matters, a small Ranch to explore, horses to ride, and a garden that Dad loved. He would invite friends over to select items from his garden and talk. A garden was essential in the country. I remember as a small boy, an old man called Bailey; he would come to our ranch with his team of mules hocked up to a wagon, with a plow in the back of it. We would talk as he unhitched the mules from the wagon and attached the plow to the mules. Then he was ready to plow and prepare the garden. He and his family lived down the way by the railroad station. There he would gather left over planking from the station to repair his home for his wife and two daughters. Old Bailey was always friendly and the two of us would talk during his break time. I can still hear Old Bailey's wagon and mules as they came down our country road. I had my work or chores to do each afternoon after school. This included checking fences for any breaks that the cattle could get through, checking on cattle and horses, and general ranch stuff. I never was paid, just doing my expected share of the workload and having a place to call home. As a man, I now know the importance of chores, and how this makes a boy grow up to man-hood. I had common sense, a mechanical mind, a strong body, and natural aptitudes for math and science, as long as I put the time into studying. This was not as easy for me as it appears; I had to burn the mid-night oil as they say. But dreams cannot be reached, without first trying.

My home was wood frame, one story, with white siding; it was about 1,000 square feet, with three bedrooms, one bathroom, a living room, a small dining room, and a kitchen, that was it.

I know that our home was small by today's standard, but we never thought of it as small, nor did we thank that we were poor, just blessed with a home full of love. My mother would have her lady friends over for coffee and a group- get together. She loved music and was always singing along with the radio.

At home one night, I was awaken by the sound of a train whistle. I set up listening to a marvelous sound that sent my mind on a journey of adventure. The train was heading for the Train Station about two miles away. There is nothing in this world, like a train blowing its whistle. I was impressed by the size and the power of the train. I would fanaticize as a boy taking a trip on this train some day. Little did I know, that later in life, I would be supporting The **NASA** Safety Center, working with Safety and Mission Assurance for Shuttle Payloads and Spacewalkers.

Mother would hang her washing on the cloth line that Dad had built for her. With Mothers assortment of clothes, now drying in the sun. Mother's family was originally from England and she had a cheerful disposition. As most mothers did back then, mothers stayed home. I can remember her encouraging my sisters and me to grow up and try new things, and not be afraid of failure. And always to follow our dreams. By the late 1950s, news about launching a satellite and the possibilities of humans traveling into space, caught my attention and gave me hope and inspiration.

My Father was an exceptional person, a man who dearly loved his family, and was proud of his Scottish heritage. He worked late hours to provide and never complained. In his shop he loved to make wood and metal objects. When he was in the Navy overseas, he would buy beautiful things for mother.

One thing he made for me and my two sisters, was a wine goblet made of silver based metal.

Ingleside Texas was a great place to grow up as a young man. Our Community had values, where one learned the value of hard work, and the importance of faith. Famililies were strong, and morals and ethics were part of the fabric of the community. They were emphasized in school, as important as science and math. We learned at an early age that faith in **God** came first and then family and community.

My best friend, Gordon Kemp lived close to the High School. His parents were of German decent. We often met up at his home and just talked about what we would like to do that day. We attended the same school and went to the same church. We were buddies true to each other. We helped each other mature over time. We even took a lot of the same math and science courses. Later Gordon and I Joined the Army Security Agency. My friend Gordon has now passed away. Two high school friends and I attended his last Service held at Ingleside, Texas.

Now I will tell you about our good neighbors, the Mathews. They were the best friends you could have. I was always going over to see this family as a young boy. As a teenager I can remember when Mr. Mathews became our local sheriff. He was good at being a sheriff, many times he was forced into shooting or wounding a suspect. He had served in WWII like my father before becoming a Sheriff. Here my father found a man he could trust and share war stories with. Mr. Mathews came home from the war with a scare on his cheek and other scares that you could not see from the war. He could not talk about the war to anyone except my Dad. He wanted to preserve his history as a sheriff, so he had a wood -smith build him a large viewing table with a glass top. He put all the weapons, handcuffs, knives and other things into it. He told the history behind each case, that he was directly involved with. Later on after he had passed away, his wife had the city move his history trove into the city museum in his name.

I was racing down the road between Ingleside and Aransas Pass, Texas when all of a sudden I heard a siren from a police car. I was scared of course, I pulled over and waited for a long time for the policemen to fuss at me for driving so fast. I had a date with a new girl and I was late. When finally the policeman approached my window, I kept saying how sorry I was for speeding. This was Mr. Jones the Justice of The Peace not an ordinary police officer; I had met this man before at my church so I knew of his duties in this County. He asked why was I speeding and I gave him my honest answer. His face went from a frond to laughing out loud. Then he said I would expect you to be at my house every Friday till you can pay off this traffic ticket. I was so happy to do what he requested, my father must never hear about me speeding and getting a ticket. This was Mr. Jones way of teaching me a lesion. I went to his home every Friday and paid an amount that we both agreed to. I will never forget this life teaching event.

My High School hired a new football coach that was young and a career minded person. He was asked later in life to join The Texas Sports Hall of Fame. He was an excellent coach who had trained under top coaches in Texas; one was The University of Texas.

Coach Emory Ballard came to our high school to coach football and teach History. I remember that day as it just happened. Everyone was introduced to our new coach, those that were interested in playing football. I was more than interested, I loved the sport. Last year I had Coach Smith for History and football. So I got picked for left End, a position that I had recently played. My jersey was number 17. All together we had a team of 34 players who were picked to play. Our team beat every team around our area, and then played High Schools outside our district, we played and won. We were the Ingleside Mustangs, powerful and strong. Coach Ballard was the one who inspired each of us to work as a team, to achieve what very few football players in The State of Texas has ever achieved.

Much later in life, my wife and I were invited to attend the Home Coming Game for the Spring Tigers in Spring, Texas. There head coach was Emory Ballard, our old Coach of Ingleside, Texas. We were to meet up with this friend and Coach. I did not know at the time, this was my last moment to see him alive. Emory Bellard had Lou Gehrigs's disease and passed away. What an honor to have played under this excellent coach for the Ingleside Mustangs.

I remember our English teacher from High School, her name was Vivian Sheldon. One could say, that she was one of my first Mentors. Miss Sheldon took an interest in me. Maybe she could see in me the potential I had, before I could. She knew about my dream to work in the Space Industry. She was always encouraging me to follow my dream. Many years later, I was invited to a ceremony at the Old Ingleside High School, now a Junior High School. This was a ceremony to name the new school after Miss Sheldon, what an honor. After the ceremony, Miss Sheldon and I were able to talk. The first thing she asked was, did I follow my dream. After all this time she had not forgotten my dream. Miss Sheldon has passed away, but not the memories of that fine and noble person still lingers.

I played football, track, and field sports in high school. I was really fast in the 440 relays. When I was thrown the ball to run for a touchdown I needed good blocking from teammates to make this happen. Our coach was responsible for our team spirit. He always emphases the impotence of working together as a unified team. I used this team spirit at **NASA** and it worked like a charm, everyone has something to contribute to the team. This team identify is strong thru out all of the Space Shuttle programs and the International Space Station (ISS).

My Boy Scout group had been invited to the world famous Jamboree held in Dallas, Texas. This event was hard to place in; but we worked hard to have our Scout group attend.

Another boy-hood story comes to life with me and three of my good friends. We drove down a sandy road at night with caution and without lights. There in the moonlight, we could hardly see our way using my Dads 1960 Ford Pickup.

Each of us had this central thought in mind; will the excitement and experience of a life time out weight all of the pain and danger that could lie ahead for us? Finally the truck came to a stop. One could taste the excitement and fear. Each of us had taken the dare of all dares, to steal watermelons from old man Fosset's melon patch. No body liked Mr. Fosset because he was evil and just plain mean. The moonlight cast an unnatural glow on the barbed wire fence, as the boys were crossing over. Each of us carefully moved about like ghostly figures in a graveyard. A shotgun blasted away, everyone thought is this a load of rock salt or lead coming our way? Scrambling to hold onto their melons, each boy sought the safety of the truck. As the last boy was tearing thru the barbed wire fence, a steel toothed wolf trap snapped missing the boy's foot by a few inches. With melons in hand, the boys needed to hurry. The truck stalled, each of us was ready to panic. Finally the truck started. We had to back up all the way out due to a narrow path. We had planed on taking our melons to the old County Cemetery, there each one of us with pounding hearts, let neverous laughter take over. When the four of us adults get together at a reunion, we remember the <u>Great Watermelon Heist.</u>

I have left out one of the important points that I would like to discuss at this time, "girls." The boy's knew on Saturday night, where to find the girls. If you were from Ingleside, you would head for Aransas, Pass Texas or Rockport, Texas. A teenage boy would not have too many choices to make.

In Aransas Pass, one would head for the "Wreck", A Community Center run by Volunteer Women. In the Wreck there were two pool tables, three games of that time, and wonderful music, the latest music for this time period.

Let the good times roll. All of the teenage girls came to dance, and they were eager to dance. The teenage boys, some were a little shy and rusty when it came to dancing. But when they played a slow tune, most everyone was at the dance floor. I can remember slow dancing was so popular to get a large group of girls and boys together, just holding each other in their arms. Songs like "*In The Still of The Night*" There was intermission, time to talk, eat food and drink, and to exchange phone numbers, addresses came later if you were lucky. I remember passing up on *The Shy Girls* .

This was a big mistake and let me tell you why. Behind most shy girls is a beautiful being just wanting to be known and appreciated. I was introduced to such a person; she changed my way of thinking. She was quite an interesting person after she would open –up to me. I found a real friend in this girl. One who could be trusted and believed that my dream was possible.

In 1958, The National Aeronautics and Space Administration (**NASA**) were created. On April 1959, NASA introduced the first US space travelers- the Mercury Seven. They were called the first "Astronauts". A term derived from two Greek words meaning "Star Sailor". There was so much excitement, in our Nation, I truly was proud of The USA. To dream of traveling into space, and I wanted to be part of this grand adventure

It was in 1962, time for our Senior Class Trip to experience a dude ranch located in Bandera, Texas. Every one of us was ready for this trip. We had talked about doing this for so long, I was wondering if it would happen at all. The day had finally arrived. Our High School had chosen this Dude Ranch for its reputation of having a lot to offer our group for activities. Several of us had already lived on a ranch, but this was different. A long line of school buses were ready to move out. Our group of students were all excited and anxious to be on our way. The drivers of the busses were teachers of ours. The students were all excited and could not be refrained from expressing them selves, of course in a good manner. The fall weather was somewhat cool and I was glad for that. The long journey had ended and we were happy to be there.

The following day was jam backed with things to experience, like horse back ridding, this was an easy one for me coming from a small ranch. Most of the boys and girls did have a look upon their face, and wondering how do I clime up on this beast. The evening gathering of all the High Schools was a sight to behold, all together there was four schools, including ours. Our Teachers and their staff laid out the guidelines for us. The game room was full of new games to play. A lot of our group had already joined in with other schools to play the games. There were girls from all over Texas to meet and I was not the least bit shy. After meeting up with several girls, one of my teachers mentioned, that I do not let grass grow under my feet. My buddies and I made friends of girls from Kaufman, Texas.

After returning home, we all got together and made plans to visit our girl friends from Kaufman, Texas. All of the girls lived close to each other and were from the same High School.

Father had bought me a 1960 Mercury Sedan. A bit old but sharp as could be. His gift to me for graduation. Having high scores in Math and Science helped also. With me providing the transpiration, now the other young man would help with expenses for the trip. After several days passed, my Mother approached me and said. We are allowing you to take this trip, but do not take us for granted. I knew what trust meant to my parents. I replied; my Faith Compass will ensure me to return home safe. My friends Gordon Kemp, James Miller, Buddy Lewis and me all came on this adventure.

The trip went smoothly and we arrived first at the home of a girl friend of Buddy Lewis. This was the Thomas household and the parents were happy to see us; and they invited us for supper. Later we all went to our lodging for the night at our Motel. Each of us all phoned our girl friends to say hi and talk about seeing them the next morning. Each girl had a car and would meet all of us at the Texas State Fair. This was an exciting time for everyone. There were so many rides to choose from, I loved most of them, but some looked dangerous to me. My girl friend wanted to have some quite time so the two of us could talk. She was concerned about how I felt about her. I was taken back a little. I finally said, I do care for you and would love to see you again. She said that she was heading for college soon, and we could write to each other. That night had a full moon overhead as we held each other tightly in our arms.

The next morning we all went to the home of the Thomas Household. We said how grateful all of us were, that you were gracious in taking us into your home and treating us like family. They replied, you are family now. We drove away that morning with a feeling of love for our new family. Later on we stopped for breakfast, each of us were ready to see our home again. I had driven for so long, I was tired and it was dark. Some one spotted a sign that read "Road Side Park Ahead" gladly I pulled in to the park and soon we fell fast asleep. Around midnight, flashlights held by two State Policeman were beaming into our car. After the policeman had our attention, they wanted us to know that we had to move on, due to a break out from the Mental Asylum across the street. We drove home very tired.

It was in 1962; time to attend Del Mar College in Corpus, Christi, Texas, I went there for two year, and was growing restless hearing all about the end of the Vietnam War and I wanted to do my part. My Father knew a friend named Tom Cox, A Mechanical Engineer who also knew about my dream of one day working at **NASA.**

This engineer used his skills as a Mentor to help me achieve my dream in life. He said, I have talked with your parents and they agree with me. My parents were not able to afford the full cost of four years of college. They had some extra money for my expenses, but that was all. The War in Vietnam was coming to a close and now was the time to enlist. Mr. Cox knew of an origination called The Army Security Agency, located at Fort Devens, Massachusetts. If I was selected, it would help me in being prepared to work for **NASA** as an employee on Department of Defense (DOD) projects, and four years of College paid for by the Army.

My friend Gordon Kemp and I went to the recruitment office in San Antonia, Texas to sign up for The Army. Both of us had a battery of tests to access if we could be sent to Fort Devens, to work for the Army Security Agency. The testing of our mental ability was hard. We survived, we made the grade.

Gordon and I were off to basic training at Fort Chaffee Arkansas. The winter was very cold, and raining. I remember having to be out in the dense forest; we would huddle up close to stay warm. I was ready to go to Fort Devens to begin training for The Army Security Agency. My good friend Gordon Kemp became very sick in basic training with the flu and was transported to the base hospital. After basic training I was to report to Fort Devens without my friend. Later on I was told that Gordon would be sent to Germany.

I served in the U.S. Army for two years at Fort Devens Massachusetts. I worked for The Army Security Agency now under The Department of Defense (DOD), I received a Top Security Classification. Later I entered College at University of Houston Clear Lake, Texas. After four years, I earned a Degree in Engineering Management. I owe all of this my Faith, my parents, and my Mentors in life that has guided me on my Journey. I was hired by Lockheed Engineering and Science corp. located at **NASA** to work in the world famous Shuttle Avionics Integration Laboratory. (SAIL) at Johnson Space Center.

On May 5, 1961, **NASA** launched the first American, Allen Shepard into space. He flew on a Mercury Space Craft; he named his capsule Freedom 7. It was launched on a Red stone Rocket. He flew 116 miles high, and then he came down. Much later in life he went to the moon on Apollo 14 as the commander and was launched from a Saturn V Rocket. He was the Chief of the Astronauts Office, he died in 1998. I am thankful for the blessing of knowing this brave Astronaut.

WAR AND SPACE ROCKETS

The snow has been falling all night and now it was a magical morning to wake up-to. I remember when I first came to Fort Devens, Mass. in the fall of 1964. I had finished my basic training at Fort Chaffee Arkansas. The war in Vietnam was coming to a close, but not before millions of Men, Women and Children were displaced or killed by this ugly war. I had signed up to serve in this war for two years, working for the Army Security Agency. I was assigned to Discyper secret code and other maters relating to The Department of Defense (DOD). At the Army Base I was required to maintain a Top Security Clearance at all times.

The Tet offensive was a coordinated attack on more than 100 cities and outposts in South Vietnam. This massive offensive shocked the American public and eroded support for the War effort. The Tet offensive marked a turning point in the war and the beginning of the slow painful American withdrawal from the region. More than 3 million people including 58,000 Americans were killed in this conflict. The war was very divisive for the Americans at home. This was the most unpopular war ever.

I would report to First Sargent Bob Fisher, who was a Native Texan like me. We made friends and Bob became a Mentor to me. As time went on, Bob learned about my dream of working for **NASA**. Bob had a friend at the Boeing Co. working for **NASA** on the Saturn V Rocket Program in New Orleans. Much later I received orders to go to Vietnam, but faith had a hand here, because my orders were cancelled due to the cutting back of troops going to Vietnam. I would remain at this Army Fort to train troops for the Army Security Agency.

The New England States were all knew to me, I experienced this beautiful country between Boston, Mass. and Bar, Harbor Maine. With the change of the seasons, the trees are the most beautiful. The apple orchards are all over this country. I have never tasted apples so diverse and truly sweet. The Army Fort was next to a small Town called Ayer, Massachusetts. There was one movie theatre, good coffee shops, and a USO Military Center which held a dance on Saturday Nights.

The Army went all out when it came to entertaining their troops. I was at the USO to have a good time dancing as well as meeting new ladies. The dance floor was always full. Most of the ladies were from the city of Boston Mass. One night, four women came to the dance from Boston. After dancing and getting to know one special lady from the group, her name was Mary. We both talked a lot about Christmas that was coming soon. When I told her that I would not be going home for Christmas, she invited me to spend Christmas Day at her Parents home. I was speechless, then I accepted her offer with much happiness. We traveled to Bar Harbor on Christmas Eve, to meet her parents and experience the true meaning of Christmas. I will forever cherish the new friendships that were made on this special day, on my journey in life.

I have traveled to Boston many times on a one-day pass to experience dining at the wonderful harbor. I enjoyed visiting and eating lobsters, for you do not get this at home. I cannot tell you in words, how this adventure has expanded my world. I am an Army Veteran forever, I am so proud.

Joe Stephens, a fellow serviceman at this Army Base invited me to go with him to his parent's home in New York City. At last I would visit this wonderful City. I was happy to take him up on his offer. Joe was a true

Italian, who had adventures in store for me. Joe and I would visit the New York Central Park first. There were so many things to see and do. Like hiking trails, biking, and even a lake to sail on. We later stopped at a Pizza shop, that my friend knew the owners. I have never tasted a real Italian Pizza until now. This was the best Pizza I have ever eaten. The next day we were off to visit the down town area of New York City. To get there we took the underground transit system. I was amazed at this tunnel built by Italians and others coming over to America. I was totally blown away, at all of the tall buildings. That evening we enjoyed a musical show. The next day we were off to visit the Statue of Liberty and the Immigration Center, I was excited to have the opportunity to experience the sights and sounds of this great city.

Joe Stephens Grandparents came over from Italy, to make a new home in America. A long time ago my Great Grandfather came from Scotland to America. As we arrived back to our Army Base, we both were filled with the fact that we were proud to be an American. Fort Devens was a small Army Post, but big in the sense of Security, so many important Army Commanders would visit here to learn the most-up-to date information on security. I am proud to have served with honor at this Army Base.

Before I left the Army, I was entertained by the Platters at our USO Center. A musical group of five singers who came to us to show their appreciation. I will never forget when I was notified, that this world famous musical group was coming to our small Army Post with Tony Williams as the lead singer.

I so enjoyed all of their songs, like "The Great Pretender." I wanted to get my fill of this place before my service time was up. So I returned to Bar Harbor Maine with my friend Mary to see this beautiful country. We visited her parents and they were happy that I took the time to say good-by. We had time to rent a small sail boat, one about eighteen feet long. With my prior sailing experience, the sailboat handled nicely. Mary and I remained good friends and we would write to each other.

I left Fort Devens in the fall of 1966 and was looking forward to visiting everyone at home. My Sargent Bob Fisher handled everything for me and I was given the name of a Boeing Engineering Manager who worked for **NASA**, at the Saturn V Rocket Facility in New Orleans.

My family was happy to see me after so long a time, and they were trilled to find out that I had landed a job supporting **NASA.**

I phoned Boeing Aerospace in New Orleans and talked with Mr. Walter Scott, an Engineering Manager in the Mechanical Design Section. He was so helpful in finding me a job. In fact, I learned later that my mentor and friend Bob Fisher had asked Walter Scott if he would hire me with my Engineering Design training and he agreed. Again it pays to have friends and Mentors who believe in you. I inquired about when to meet with Mr. Scott and where would he suggest I find lodging while I worked at the Saturn V Facility. He suggested an Apartment Complex that was new and just a few miles from the Saturn V Complex. After phoning the Apartment Complex, I selected a one-bed room apartment. The manager was also helpful, he assured me that I would fit in nicely with the people who live here.

On Monday morning I had arrived at **NASA**, first thing was to get a parking sticker and my Security badge, I had taken a course in Mechanical Design at Del Mar College. This was my ticket to working for Boeing Aerospace and with help from my friend Bob Fisher. I was then taken to meet Mr. Walter Scott. A kind man, with experience and appreciation for his job. It was almost noontime and he suggested that we go to the Cafeteria to have lunch. Later on we went to meet my new Supervisor, a Mr. Tom Emmerson who was 45 years of age and with a sense of humor. He welcomed me into his group, and explained to me about my duties. He later took me to meet the Manager of the Machine Shop. I learned all about the shop and how important it was to give them good accurate drawings for the machinist.

I knew this was my first Job supporting **NASA** and I was so proud. Back then all mechanical designers, were what we Call- on the board design. We did our work with special paper, and special lead. Place the paper on the board and draw your parts to scale or in 1/10 scale. Times have changed, now all drawings are computer generated. I have such a drawing of the first stage of the Saturn V Rocket. Signed by all of the Mechanical Designers and Management. I will always valuable this gift from so many close friends. I will present it my book.

At work I put myself into the job that lay ahead of us all, to turn out drawings to be made into machined parts for the First Stage S-1C of The Saturn V Rocket. We all took measurements at the site of the first stage, so that, the parts we were to draw were accurate. This meant climbing around the structure. I enjoyed the work even if it was hard at times

I made it back to my apartment full of pride and a little tired. There was a rumor going around that we were due to start over time. I did not mind, I could use the extra money. That evening I went to the pool for a little swimming. There were all sorts of people from the apartment having fun. After some time I set next to a young lady getting a Sun tan. We introduced each other, her name was Nancy. We talked about the day and about a dance that was to be at our apartment. Nancy was visiting a girl friend; she was from Baton Rogue Lousiana.

The Saturn V Facility came under the management of **NASA** in 1961. Boeing was responsible to **NASA** for detailed design, fabrication, and assembly, of the first stage S-1C. The Rockets used on the Saturn V were developed by Rocketdyne Corp. The Saturn V used 5 rockets to boast it into Space. Boeing was also responsible to **NASA** for Systems Engineering, and Mission Support. The entire Saturn V Program had a large responsibility to **NASA.**

Boeing had full responsible for the first stage of the Saturn V. Tom Emmerson took me out where the work for the **S-IC** was being built. It was the largest vehicle I could imagine, and it was held in a vertical position to work on. Mr. Emmerson explained that I would be utilized as a Mechanical Designer on The First Stage (S-IC). Mr. Emmerson explained about the other Corporations involved in the production of the Saturn V Rocket. For the Second stage was to be built in California by North American Corp and for the third stage, to be built in California by Mc Donnell Douglas Corp.

The three-stage rocket, liquid –fueled super heavy-lift launch vehicle. Was developed to support the Apollo program for human exploration of the Moon and was later used to launch Skylab, the first American Space Station. The Saturn V was launched 13 times from the Kennedy Space Center with no loss of crew or payload. As of 2017, The Saturn V remains the tallest, heaviest, and most powerful rocket in the world. Holds records for the heaviest payload. This Saturn V Rocket was designed under the direction of Wernher Von Braun and Arthur Rudolph at the Marshall Space Flight Center in Huntsville, Alabama. To date, the Saturn V remains the only launch vehicle to launch missions to carry humans beyond low earth orbit. A total of 24 Astronauts were launched to the Moon, three of them twice, in the four years spanning December 1968 through December 1972.

I was excited, a rumor had started about the famous Wernher Von Braun was to visit our site here at **NASA**. I came to work thinking, what luck will I have of meeting this man. Later in the day I was coming out of the first stage of the Saturn V rocket, with drawings in hand. There he stood, looking at me, I just had to meet this great man. I shook his hand and said how pleased I am to meet you, He smiled at me and asked my name. Then he said; "one day when all the stages are complete, we are going to the Moon". Then he hurried away to join his group. I will never forget that day. Later in my career the two of us had another chance meeting at The Marshall Space Center in Huntsville, Alabama. I will cover this in detail in a chapter later on.

After the Rockets were test fired and approved. The entire first stage of the S-IC Rocket was shipped by barge from Lousiana to The Kennedy Space Center in Florida. Here all three sections were mated together at a special hanger at Kennedy Space Center.

The Saturn V Rocket first launch was on Nov. 9, 1967. It was a three Stage rocket at a diameter of 33 feet, with a height of 363 feet. It weighted more than 6 million pounds. The Propulsion for stage 1 was 7.5 million pounds, for stage 2, I million pounds. For stage 3, 200,000 pounds total.

Let us put the Saturn V Rocket in perceptive, it was the height of a 36 –story- tall –building and 60 feet taller than the Statute of Liberty. When fully fueled for lift-off, the Saturn V weighted 6.2 million pounds and generated 7.6 million pounds of trust at lift-off.

The Saturn V Rocket used all 3 stages for the Apollo missions. Each Stage would burn its engines until it was out of fuel. And would then separate from the rocket. The engines on the next stage would fire, and the rocket would continue into space. The first stage had the most powerful engines, since it had the challenging task of lifting the fully fueled rocket off the ground. The first stage that I worked on lifted the rocket to an altitude of about 42 miles. The second stage carried it from there almost into Orbit. The third stage placed the Apollo Spacecraft into earth orbit and pushed it toward the Moon. The first two stages fell into the ocean after separation. The third stage either stayed in Space or burned up in the Astrosphere.

A group of us would head for the City of New Orleans to see the French Quarter, to dine and hear the best Jazz in the world. I was introduced to the wonderful flavors of Cajon cooking. I began to like gumbo, and the special flavored seafood. The music in the Quarter is usually loud, but one can find a calmer more satisfying music. I even found a church in the middle of all of this, a small white building that catered to the poor. It was called The Church of the Salvation Army. This little church came alive, as the chorus sang old gospel music, and I smiled.

The old streetcar was swaying back and forth on the tracks. This was the oldest streetcar in the city. The St. Charles Line; it was taking us on a historical journey. The streetcar was very old, with mahogany seats, brass fittings and exposed ceiling light bubs. This old streetcar symbolizes the charm and romance of this great city. Swaying along through a tunnel of live oaks. The streetcar passes dozens of antebellum mansions, historical monuments, and Audubon Zoological Gardens. That is what Nancy and I came to see. We had packed a lunch for us to eat later under a moss-covered tree. We enjoyed each other's company and remained close friends.

Overtime had started, some were happy for the extra pay, while others were grumbling about having to work late. The overtime, I have to admit, was a change in my working habits. The reason behind the overtime was because Wernher Von Braun was not happy with the scheduling for the completion date. We had to play catch-up. As a young man this was fine with me as I adjusted to the new schedule. Working later meant having more time to get to know my fellow workers. I met the most interesting man, he was originally from Russia, and his name was Rubin. I was working on a drawing and asked his opinion; his accent was foreign to me. He then said young man I am from Russia. I came to this country as a young boy many years ago. At lunch break I set by this interesting man too learn more. He felt like talking, explaining about trouble in Russia. I listened intensely to learn more about this person. I may ask too many questions, so I backed off real quick understanding his privacy. He introduced me to Borsch, a Russian stew with intense aroma He was enjoying for lunch. Later in The afternoon we had a chance to talk on our break. He told me about the trouble in Russia, He still had relatives living there, but food was scarce.

The weekend was finally here, it was time to relax. The dance was packed, the music was loud, and the atmosphere was great. Nancy was a good dancer, I so enjoyed myself. After the dance Nancy and I had time along, her French perfume was intoxicating.

I knew that the time was getting Close to when I would be leaving. But I did not think it would come so fast. I have so many new friends to be thankful for and I have learned to design vital parts for The Saturn V Rocket.

On the last month, I went on a sailing adventure in Lake Poncetrain, in New Orleans. The lake was beautiful with a good breeze blowing. There were three of us in a racing sailboat. The boat with large sails was eager to race. We trimmed the sails just right and off we went to win the race. We were all happy that we won. But sorrow and sadness would put a damper on our victory.

My close friend William Jenkins who worked at the Saturn V Facility with me was a good person, with a passion for life. He was about my age, but with a heaver build. We heard screaming coming from people further down the lake. My friend was in the water trying to save a teenager that went overboard from a sailboat. William tried his best fighting to save the frightened teenager. He had a heart attack. Other boats in the area came to their rescue, but too late for William, He was dead when he was dragged from the lake. I felt empty inside, as I said good by to a dear friend.

On Monday morning I came to **NASA** to say good-by to all my friends, and to every security guard who saw me come and go for one year.

I took time to say how much I appreciated each one of them. Then I went in to see my Project Manager, Mr. Walter Scott to say good-by. Mr. Scott was in a good mood as usual. He shook my hand and said he was proud of me starting college, he also said that he will miss my positive attitude.

Then he said, I have your work progress report, which he signed. I so appreciated his guidance and help during my stay here at **NASA**. He was a friend to me, but much more, he cared about my future. He was well aware of my dream. He said that Tom Emmerson was waiting for me to visit his department for the last time.

Tom with a gleam in his eyes presented me with a drawing of the First Stage of the Saturn V Rocket, with signatures of all the Management and every one of my friends that I had worked with. I was so taken back, these Signatures were so precious to me, and will remain so forever. I will present the **drawing with *my friend's signatures in my book*.**

Tom and I exchanged hugs along with so many of my friends. We also exchanged mailing addresses, this was before e-mail. I promised to keep in touch and stay out of trouble. I had one more person that I had to say good-by to a second time. Her name was Virginia Bell, a close friend who was helpful and thoughtful. She and I had the same last name, our ancestors were from Scotland and she was my Engineering lead on projects.

I was cleared through Security and it was the final time to say good-by to every one. I looked around the facility, one last time. I though about the time I had spent here along-side my friends and now I was heading back home to Texas.

As I was heading home and driving for some time, I thought about all that had transpired while working for **NASA** and living in New Orleans. Is there a path already laid out for each of us. I pondered this question over and over. Yes, in my case I was on a journey to work for **NASA**, and I was following my dream.

It has been a long journey, I have been truly blessed, I long to see my friends and family at home. They say home is where the heart is, I agree.

My parents were so proud of me getting ready to start my first semester at college, I will visit them soon with a glad heart and thankful that my service in the Army will pay for my college tuition. I had saved up from working at **NASA** enough to pay for my housing and other expenses, for about 18 months. My parents will help also with my expenses so it looks like it is all up to me to excel in college and continue to follow my dream.

COLLEGE AND MOON MISSIONS

I entered The University of Houston-Clear Lake in the spring of 1967 when things were heating up between Russia and United States. Most large colleges were so against the war in Vietnam and started to show their disapproval. This was a time of social upheaval. A lot of Americans did not agree with the war in Vietnam. There also were those who agreed. There were those for democracy and human rights overseas, and there was some Americans fighting for civil rights issues at home. Our campus was close to **NASA**, which inspired the students who may work there one day. It has a good curriculum for an Engineering Management Degree. I chose this degree program because it would allow me to supervise people in a team setting, to use administrative skills to solve problems. I would work with product design and develop systems and processes for engineering. I also would work in research and design, coordinate the development for production, quality control, and testing for new products. Also work with Safety Engineering and Systems Engineering analyst.

I was looking forward to making new friends in college. This college was what I was looking for in size and location, and I can use my GI Bill to pay for my classes. You had to be a native Texan and go to a college in Texas. I had met my requirements, thanks to the Army, my mentors, and my faith.

In the spring of 1967 I signed up for my freshman year. This summer was very successful for **NASA**. In 1967 Gemini 9 with Gene Cernan and

Tom Stafford and Gemini 10 flew with John Young and Mike Collins. The first Apollo mission was slated for February 1967. I wanted a part of this grand adventure. I had already worked for **NASA** and my mind was racing, it was hard to compose myself.

My parents came to visit before I started college, they were happy for me, and I promised to call them soon. Without their guidance and help along the way, I would not be here. I moved into an apartment complex, like I did in New Orleans. The apartment was close to the college, and I had my car. My classes were all assessable by walking to help with expenses. I met a friend at college to share my two bedroom apartment. His name is Charles White, a native Texan; I have come to admire his love for life. Charles would join our study group at college. This apartment was full of college students. I was blessed to find a college friendly apartment close to the University.

At the first day of class our Professor laid out his rules and operating procedures. He would take notice if we were not taking good notes. If one takes good notes, He or She can study, and prepare for what was coming. He said, do not let me catch you napping, or talking out of turn. That was plain and simple. I took this man at his word and this aided me in other classes.

I was not afraid of Engineering, but I was afraid of keeping up with my grades. I did not want to take on something bigger than I could handle. I sure did not want to disappoint my self or my parents either. Later that evening at the library I had time alone to think. I arose the next morning with more confidence in myself, to study with a purpose, to graduate in four or less years. I have already gained credits toward an Engineering Management Degree from Del Mar College.

My basic training in the Army, made a man of me, I had to grow up fast and forget the life that I had become acustomated to, and train with war hardened soldiers that had fought in Vietnam. I had to learn from others, and this action prepared me for the Future.

My time working at the Saturn V Complex at New Orleans helped me to organize and plan ahead. It also helped me in my field of Engineering. I had my **faith compass** to keep me headed in the right direction and goals to pursue. I missed my friends at the Saturn V Complex. When I had time I would write to Mr. Tom Emmerson to say hi and asked about the news there. The Saturn V Rocket was on schedule and everyone was working hard to build the worlds biggest, tallest, and the most powerful Rocket in the world. One day it would launch the Apollo Mission into Space. I can honestly say that I played my part in its completion. It was nearing the end of my first semester, which was a major challenge for me. I must do better next semester to keep a good grade average. **NASA** is looking for college students with excellent grades through out their college years.

I received a recipe from my old friend Rubin, from Russia who worked for Boeing at The Saturn V Complex. This was an excellent Russian Stew, and I made a large bowl of this great tasting stew called Borsch.

To advance in college, it is very important to have an excellent study group. One that is dependable and is determined to make good grades. I looked the college over for such a group and found one. This group of Engineering Management students wanted to make a difference, to work at **NASA.** I was accepted into this group of determined women and men. We would meet every other day in the library. If one was absent they were given the study notes of that meeting, but being absent too many times and you are dismissed from this group.

The second semester was asking more from me than the first semester.

I figured this would happen due to the math and science. I started to doubt my self, but I lifted my self up after talking with a lady in my study group. Her name was Shannon, a lovely person with a comforting manner about her. She said, thank of why you are here. I smiled after a while and replied, I am here to finish college first, and then go on to work for **NASA.**

Shannon also had a dream; she wanted first to finish college also, so that she could work for **NASA** in the field of Computer Science. We must help each other to achieve or goal. You could say, that we were attracted to each other.

I did not study all of my time in college; I also had free time to have some fun. I found so many things that are of interest to me, like dancing, sailing, eating out, flag football, and baseball to name a few. I was never one to drink a lot of liquor, a social drinker, you could say. When I was in New Orleans, La I experienced a lot of people drinking to excess at dances, this was not my style.

The study group at college had a free weekend and everyone was anxious to get to the beach in Galveston, Texas, to spend the day, eating seafood, and having fun. Shannon came along with the group, I was happy to see her. The temperature was warming up nicely. As we drove the I-45 freeway to Galveston, Several girls including Shannon was signing to the music on the radio. The beach was already getting crowded with people. Everyone went to change into their bathing suits. When Shannon came out of the dressing room, I admired how she looked in her bathing suit so tall and trim. I want to tell you that I am not a man beyond looking at a beautiful woman, but it is <u>how you look that counts</u>. One should never stare at a lady. We enjoyed our selves so much with swimming, walking the beach, and just talking. I remember long ago as a young boy on this beach, I am now a man.

It was during my second semester that **NASA** had high hopes for the first manned Apollo flight to the Moon. On January 27, 1967, veteran Astronaut, Ed White, Virgll "Gus" Grissom, and rookie Roger Chaffee were sitting atop the launch pad for a pre-launch test when a fire broke out in their Apollo 1 capsule, killing all three. This set the Apollo missions on hold until a full investigation into what caused this fatal accident. All Apollo missions were suspended for 20 months. This was big news in the Houston area; everyone was saddened at losing three Astronauts. Everyone was asking what happened and why and the family of the Astronauts needed help also.

The investigation board found out that an electrical spark ignited the pure oxygen in the capsule. This was changed. Also they discovered that the plug door hatch, which could not be opened against the higher internal pressure of the cabin, prevented the Astronauts rescue. The Saturn V Moon Rocket continued on schedule. I know that Mr. Emmerson and my friends working on the Saturn V project were glad for their Jobs and sad for the three brave Astronauts who perished in the fire. And this was the **first** of three tragedies in the history of **NASA.**

Towards the end of my second year the Engineering students were happy and ready to head home to visit family and friends. A majority of students were from Texas but others were out of state. The college campus was beautiful with a large acreage of trees and lakes. I too was headed home to visit family and friends. I always enjoyed Christmas, this was a time for the family to get together and celebrate the birth of Christ. My parents and grandparents would cook all the Christmas Dinner with all of the trimmings. No store bought easy to fix job, just a lot of love went into everything. On Christmas Eve we opened all of the presents with laughter and joking. I sit back and just watched, as this Christmas un-folded into a very cozy and relaxing time for all of us. This was a wonderful time to be together. My sister Joann asked me, "do you have a girl friend", I replied of course.

Astronaut Joe Allen was chosen in-group no. 6 in the year of 1967 to be with a group of Astronauts that were engineers and scientists. **NASA** had in the past chosen mainly test pilots. Joe Allen became my good friend when I supported **NASA**. He was in several Missions as a Spacewalker that I helped to support with Safety Engineering to enable him to be successful with his Spacewalks. Time was coming when more Engineers and Scientist were chosen. I have his signature on a **NASA** picture he gave me.

My Counselor and Mentor at College was successful in getting me an Internship at **NASA**. But later on, she found out that I would not be an intern for **NASA** at this time, because of politics dealing with President Nixon. A freeze on hiring interns was in effect. But an outstanding Corporation, Lockheed Martin, was now looking for Engineering Interns at Space Center Houston. Our **Lord** can close a door then open another one. I was humbled. With my extra credits from Del Mar College I was able to graduate in less than four years. I had a good grade average and intended to keep the pace going. When I enrolled in this college, I was introduced to my Counselor; she became my friend and mentor her name was Kathleen. Our study group has been a blessing to all of us. Now it was up to me to keep focused, and keep a good GPA.

Let me began with Apollo 8, because of the historical importance. This mission was launched on December 21, 1968 with Commander Frank F. Borman, Pilot James A. Lovett, Lunar Module Pilot William A. Anders. This was the first mission to be launched by the Saturn V Rocket. There were much political unrest in Europe and the United States at this time. This mission also paved the way for the Apollo 11. Apollo 8 crew members flew around the moon, an on their fourth orbit were able to take the Worlds famous photo named Earthrise. This photograph taken by William Anders of the Earth rising behind the moon was selected by Life Magazine as the photo that changed the world. Another first was the reading of the **Bible** from **Genesis** by each crew member, a biblical creation story of our earth. Borman finished the broadcast by wishing a Merry Christmas to everyone on earth. "And from the crew of Apollo 8, we close with good night, good luck, a Merry Christmas and God Bless all of you on the good earth".

On July 16, 1969, Apollo 11 lifted off for the first lunar landing mission. On July 20, 1969 The LM – with astronauts Neil A, Armstrong and Edwin E Aldrin – landed on the lunar surface while Michael Collins Orbited

overhead in the Apollo command module. Armstrong set foot on the surface, telling the million of listeners that it was "one small step for man-one
giant leap for mankind." Aldrin soon followed him out and the two plodded
around the landing site and planted an American flag. They later collected
samples of soil and rock. After more than 21 hours on the lunar surface,
they returned to Collins on board "Columbia," The next day they began
the return trip to Earth, "splashing down" in the Pacific on July 24, 1969.

Landing on the moon at what cost for Neil Armstrong and his wife
Janet. They are doing everything they can to heal their 2-year old daughter
of a brain tumor. An aeronautical engineer and industrious aviator, Neil
is a man who can almost fix anything. But he can't fix his daughter Karen,
whose death – ultimately fuels his passion to reach the moon. What really
puzzles me, is the absence of any acknowledgement of **God** or faith, par-
ticularly the Christianity of Buzz Aldrin. The first man on the moon may
have been Neil Armstrong, but the first meal on the moon was the **Lord's**
Supper. This is not mentioned, but shortly after landing on the moon, and
after Neil Armstrong had set foot on the moon, Buzz Aldrin said over the
radio " I'd like to take this opportunity to ask every person listening in, whoever and wherever they may be, to pause for a moment and contemplate the
events of the past few hours and to give thanks in his or her own way." He
then observed thanksgiving his way, by taking out a small communion kit
that had been prepared by the Webster, Texas, Presbpterian Church. There
he served as an Elder. Aldrin describes the surreal scene this way. "I reached
into my personal preference kit and pulled out the communion elements
along with a three-by-five card on which I had written the words of **Jesus**. "I
am the vine, you are the branches, whoever remains in me, an I in him, will
bear much fruit, for you can do nothing without me". Then I poured a thim-
bleful of wine from a sealed plastic container into a small chalice, and waited
for the wine to settle down in the one-sixth Earth gravity of the moon. I

silently read the bible passage as I partook of the wafer and the wine, and offered a private prayer for the task at hand and the opportunity I had been given. Neil Armstrong did not join Aldrin in taking communion; thought he respectfully observed, while Aldrin took the elements.

The U.S. Govt. along with **NASA** at the time would not make public the account of Aldrins reading the bible or taking of the elements of our Lords last Supper. Aldrin also read Psalm's 8-3-4 over a radio broadcast on the return voyage. Neil Armstrong was about landing on the moon, while Aldrin was about both, landing on the moon and the reminder of our **Lords** glory and his creation of the Universe**.**

Let me cover Splash down Parties, This party was held in celebration of the Astronauts splashing down in the Pacific Ocean. The whole world would cover this event in the news. What an ending to all the Astronauts coming home safe in their Apollo Capsule. But for Apollo 11, the world celebrated the missions end, but the crew didn't go to a party, or attend the celebrations in the streets that erupted around the country. They were quarantined, separated from the world till August 3. **NASA** was not taking any chances, back then no one knew if they had Space Sickness. President Nixon was there when the quarantined was over to greet them. The Ticker-tape parade through New York City was on August 13.

From then on the celebrations began with each splash down. Clear Lake knew how to throw a party. Curtain areas were blocked off to allow for the parties in the streets to begin. The taverns were happy for this event, everyone was drinking to celebrate. My roommate and I went to celebrate and have a beer to drink. Crowds could get a little carried away at the bars.

For this Moon landing, An Extravaganza was held at the Astrodome in Houston, Texas on August 16, 1969. The Performers for this prestigious time in history were Frank Sinatra, Master of Ceremonies, with Nancy Ames, Buddy Brock and his Orchestra, Bill Dana, Marguerite Piazza, Dionne war

Wick, and Flip Wilson I was there to celebrate also with friends from **NASA**. Neil Armstrong introduced all of the Astronauts; Closing Remarks were from Dr. Robert R. Gilruth. After all of the celebration, it was time to head for home, get up early and meet at college with my study group.

I joined the First United Methodist Church in Clear Lake Tex. after I had settled in, mainly because it has the best singles ministry in the area. This church was solid as they come. The singles had groups by age; there were three groups in the church. I belonged to the young adults. The church had sponsored group events that included trips to Galveston, and a singles ministry located in Houston. There was a young pastor assigned to all of the singles. We were assigned to helping out singles that need a hand in moving plus other things like helping single ladies with car repairs. I found out singles move a lot. Also the ladies would cook breakfast for all of the guy's. The church used Laity Lodge, a singles ministry for Christian Renewal in Kerrville Tex.

My time at the college was nearing its end of the third year, I will be a senior soon. I remember going on a singles retreat to a campground located north of Conroe, Texas. I needed to get away with this group of singles.

We had a diverse group of single men and women, some had never camped out before. This will be a time of love it or hate it. The first night, the temperature was falling and everyone was getting close to the bon fire and it was starting to rain. I had brought me and old cot, lots of blankets, and a tarp to tie onto the top of my car and let it hang down, I would use poles to support it. That night several singles had moved their cots under my shelter to stay warm and dry. There was little talk, everyone was tired and looking forward to hiking in the morning, for the rain had stopped.

A country morning has a magic charm, like no other time of day. It is a time for thought and reflection; perhaps **God** planned it that way. We were on a hiking trip into the woods, a trail allowed us to go deep into the forest. It seems that nature takes a big, deep breathe and time stands still for a while. As I listen to the voices of the morning, Nature speaks to my soul, and I smile. I have been noticing a lady with red hair that enjoyed hiking almost as much as I do, her name was Karen. We had a long talk as we were resting from the long hike. She lived in a town close to Clear Lake Tex. and worked for IBM at **NASA**. Noticing that I was without a tent, she invited me to stay with her and her son while we were at base camp. I agreed because I needed shelter for the night. She and her son, a young boy about seven years old became good friends to me.

The next day we went hiking in a different area to see the Great Lake in the forest. The next morning we broke camp after breakfast, Karen and I had a long talk to tell each what we had in common and left the door open for further conversations. I was thankful for this lady and her son. We headed for the nearest town for lunch and then home.

In November of 1969, NASA launched Apollo 12 with Astronauts Charles Conrad, Richard Gordon, and Alan Bean. Their mission was to land on the Moon for a second time. They landed near the Surveyor 3 landing site. They spent 7.5 hours walking on the surface, including an inspection of the Surveyor probe.

It was hard getting up on Monday morning after the camping trip to head for college this spring, I knew I would be working for Lockheed as an Intern. Our study group was busy, knowing that each of us had to finish with a great GPA. I could not fail now; I needed courage and faith to see me through.

In April 1970 was the flight of Apollo 13. The Apollo crew named their LM Aquarius; this title was from the song by a group called the 5th Dimension. The songs signature words, "This is the dawning of the Age of Aquarius," was picked up by the Apollo 13 crew and controllers. Symbolized the first mission of the new decade as well as the challenge and excitement of the risky lunar missions. This was one of the near disasters of the Apollo Program. At 56 hours into the flight, an oxygen tank in the Apollo service module ruptured and damaged several of the power, electrical, and life support systems. People were watching and praying all over the world, and hoping for the best. Astronaut Jim Lovell commanded the mission, Fred Haise was the LM pilot, and Jack Swigert all were well on their way to the Moon with no way of returning until they went around it. NASA personnel quickly determined that sufficient air, water, and electricity did not exist in the Apollo capsule to sustain the three Astronauts until they could return to Earth, they found that the LM-a self –contained spacecraft unaffected by the accident –could be used as a "lifeboat" to provide austere life support for the return trip. It was a close –run thing, but the crew returned safely on April 17, 1970. I want to explain; it was a combined effort by *NASA, Lockheed, Boeing, plus others*, supporting the safe return of Apollo 13. Team effort was used to find the ways and means to get the Astronauts safely home. Gene Kranz was the lead Flight Director of Mission Control who came up with the words needed to convey his feelings when there was doubt and confusion if they were able to get the Astronauts safety back, Gene Kranz said "Failure is not an option." This is a common saying now to represent any thing in fear of failure. I have also used this same description of failure.

My College Counselor and Mentor Miss Kathleen was in contact with Lockheed Martin Corp. to secure my internship for the summer of 1970. She choose this company because they were supporting **NASA** with large contracts. I did my research and was well pleased to be selected as an intern.

I arrived at Lockheed Martin Corp to meet with Mr. Roy Wilcox. He would be my coach and mentor this summer. This company was known for it's hiring of engineering students as interns. I was blessed to be considered as an intern so that I could advance my career into the future of technology and creativity. One could develop new systems to

be deployed in space, cyberspace, or for the military Department of Defense (DOD). You could help design and manufacture breakthrough products for space to aid the Spacewalkers. I will be exposed to a wealth of knowledge and experience. And very likely be hired full –time, at Lockheed Martin. I will do my best to get hired full time.

My Space Odyssey, up to know has been everything that I could ask for. A journey of faith has taken me from a young boy looking up at the Moon, to supporting **NASA** Space Programs. I was eager to begin working toward developing new processes to further Space exploration. My experience in mechanical design and working with the Department of Defense on the Saturn V Program was helpful to being hired full time later on in my internship.

At Lockheed I began a series of assignments as a member of a project management team in the flight planning and Procedures Branch under the Flight Operations Directorate. Flight missions require a large library of procedures so astronauts know exactly how to perform their tasks, ranging from assembling and using robots to changing electronic and mechanical devices. My team manages how those procedures can be accessed by the crew and/or the Mission Control Center through the use of software applications to ensure they may read and navigate through the procedures efficiently and effectively. I had to create test plans and training materials.

While being Introduced to so many new things that I have newer been exposed to before, I understandably felt a little overwhelmed. However I retraced my steps of my Faith Journey, and I quickly learned to adapt to this new environment and went forward to execute my professional self with Quality and Mission Assurance.   As a new team member, I learned to adapt in this new environment and impressed my Coach and Mentor Roy Scott. I had joined a team of professional Engineers and Designers while at the Saturn V Project. I learned to be a team member, this meant committing yourself to the team's purpose and agenda. So this has helped me at Lockheed. My mentor helped me to execute professional work and noticed how I interacted with my fellow team members. I must always believe in my self and not doubt the task that lies ahead of us. The summer of 1970 was coming to an end; I would graduate in the fall and then hope for the best. I did not have to wait long, my College Councilor Miss Kathleen let me know that Mr. Roy Scott; from Lockheed Martin had contacted her with good news.

I had been selected to start work, full time with Lockheed Martin. The fall semester had started and my study group was busy as always. Some of my friends were hired as interns this past summer also.

The last semester of college was a challenge as well as a relief to know that I would be supporting **NASA**.

Our study group was hard at work helping us to maintain our GPA and having a little break also.

I dearly cared for this dedicated group of people, who have given so much to each other. At the end of the semester when we were given our grade average, everyone celebrated. After we graduated, we through a party of all parties, now we had to say good by to each other and start a new chapter in our lives. Most were Texans, so that makes it easy to keep in touch. I was ready to start on my Faith and Space Journey at **NASA.**

Chapter 4

THE APOLLO MISSIONS AND SKYLAB

I was now working for **NASA** full time at The Johnson Space Center in 1970. Being an intern was another step in my space and faith journey. After all these years with so many set backs, trials, and finishing college, I am finally working for **NASA** Apollo Missions. I was introduced to Mr. Bob Jones, an Engineering Professional for new hires at Lockheed Martin Corporation. He was a likeable person and I could tell that we would work well together. Bob first off, wanted me to read and know all of Lockheed Martin procedures dealing with **NASA**. Then later on, he would introduce me to several different Departments. The first two days was to let me become relaxed and learn the ins and outs of this huge Corporation. As a new hire I wanted to make a good impression, not only for Bob, but everyone that I came in contact with. I was starting my Journey alongside many talented people that had a dream also. We were a unified group of employees, all working together as a team to achieve our space journey. I was put into the Engineering Department because of my degree plan of Engineering, and for work on The Saturn V Project. The Company was pleased that I had already worked with **NASA** and knew what was expected of me. After a week, I felt at ease in developing new hardware for the Apollo Project. A launch was to take place in January for the Apollo 14 mission. This launch was so important because of what transpired with the Apollo 13 mission. **NASA** and Lockheed employees worked to make sure this will never happen again, (failure is not an option).

Rumors were flying thought out **NASA,** and the news was mixed. A Space Task Group headed by the chairmanship of Vice President Spiro T. Agnew was to plot a course for the future of the Apollo Space Program. The politics of this effort was intense. **NASA** lobbed hard with this group for a far-reaching post-Apollo Space Program that included development of a space station, a reusable Space Shuttle, a Moon base, and a human expedition to Mars. **NASA** was clear on what they wanted, but President Nixon did not act on **NASA'S** recommendations. **NASA'S** budget had been cut from a high of $5.9 billion to $4.25 billion. President Nixon zeroed in on a single aspect of the Von Braun paradigm for future space exploration developing the Shuttle. This marked a key shift in **NASA's** charter from Space exploration to space utilization. Meanwhile Nixon now was going to cut **NASA'S** budget to $3.4 billion. All of the employees working at **NASA** were up-set. I knew that layoffs were coming, that was certain because of the budget cut. About this same time a hiring freeze was in force. I prayed that this not be the end of my space journey. I believe that **God** has a plan for each of us. I do believe that we are here for a purpose. I also believe that we cannot leave it all up to **God**. You have to be willing to work hard yourself. One cannot give up easily; one must carry on and work with a plan to succeed. Dreams that we all carry can happen in unexpected ways We must press onward to reach our **God** driven goals.

January 31, 1971 Apollo 14 was launched on a rainy day on top of a Saturn V Rocket. This mission was the third U.S. lunar landing mission. With Alan B Shepard, and Edgar Mitchell went to the Moon while Stuart Roosa piloted the CM. (Command Module) They were able to perform nine hours of moonwalks and brought back 98 pounds of lunar material. Alan B Shepard was much older and the lease experienced. He was chosen as one of the first Astronauts of the Mercury Seven. He was the first American into Space making a 16-minute flight in the Mercury capsule Freedom Seven. Alan B Sheppard was pledged with an inner ear problem, which caused him to retire from the Space Program. None of Apollo 14 crew would ever fly in space again; each Astronaut went into private business.

I was heading for work when I came up on a stranded motorist, and I pulled over to the side of the road and proceeded to ask Irene in the car if she needed any help. She recognized me from work, and said that a wrecker was on the way to tow the car and could she have a ride with me to Lockheed Martin. I said hop in and we watched as her car was being towed by the wrecker. Irene and I had met before, when I was introduced to her Boss, Mr. Brown. I was new in the department and Mr. Brown and I talked briefly about his Engineering Department. I did not know at this time of my Space Journey, but Mr. Brown would take me under his guidance and be a <u>Mentor to me</u>. I would learn the value of this great Manager, and his effort to help employees get ahead. Everyone at this company honored him. He was a noted Professional Engineering Manager. My chance meeting with Irene, that morning was a faithful gift that would keep on giving.

One week later, I was called into a meeting with Mr. Brown; he explained the situation with Lockheed and **NASA** concerning layoffs. I was to report to a new manager Mr. Robert Downing. I was saved and I said a prayer under my breath. A Lockheed Manager had asked for me to come and work for his origination. I was assigned to work at the Shuttle Avionics Integration Laboratory (SAIL). It was the only facility for the Apollo Program and later used for The Space Shuttle Program where actual orbiter hardware and flight software can be integrated and tested in a simulated flight environment. It supported the entire Space Shuttle program to perform integrated verification tests. It also contained Firing Room Launch Equipment identical to that used at Kennedy Space Center (KSC). Thus complete ground verification as well as countdown and abort operations could be tested and simulated.

What an honor too be picked for this world renewed facility at **NASA** Johnson Space Center**.** I was thrilled, and thankful that people that cared about me, and remembered my name. With the end of the Apollo Era coming soon, and the start up work on the new Space Shuttle to take Astronauts into Space. I will lead a team of dedicated members to finish the Apollo Missions to the Moon and start work on the up-in coming transition to the Space Shuttle.

I had been planning a camping trip with friends, we would go to Inks Lake camp grounds. We arrived in the late afternoon to pitch our tents and get squared away. After dinner it was getting dark early, a large thunder storm was coming our way. We were busy putting things up before the storm hit. After we were safety into our tents, we heard a terrible sound, lighting had knocked down a large pine tree close to my tent. We were all scared, then came the heavy rain and thunder. The group worried throughout the night. Finally morning came, we had made it. We still remember this camping trip till this day.

It was time to visit the machine shop of **NASA** to check on how my machined parts were doing for the next Apollo Mission. At this time I will meet the Manager of Scheduling, Mr. Tom Davis for all work at this huge machine shop at Johnson Space Center. I have always respected the knowledge that is required for a machinist, the work is persist, and he or she must read the drawings and produce a machined part or parts to close tolerances. I learned so much from each dedicated machinist. Shop Manager Tom Davis and I hit it off right away. Tom was a kind and generous man, which impressed me. I had time to visit some dedicated machinists and I noticed while at the **NASA** machine shop, that a lot of material was being wasted. I studied how to better save on material after machining was finished. I turned my Cost Saving Report into my new manager Mr. Robert Downing. After some time, Mr. Downing called me into his office and shook my hand, my plan was approved and I was very happy. After this I was always looking for any cost saving plan that could save money for the company or to help **NASA** prosper. A close friend who worked at **NASA** once said to me; always look for ways to help out the company you work for, without expecting a reward. I pondered his advice, and finally learned to become active in serving my company, in volunteering, and helping out when and where I was needed. This has helped me in so many ways, to be recognized. So many times an employee seeks a money reward, but the greatness lies in serving the company.

The company picnic was another way to volunteer and it was going to be held soon. I joined the group of volunteer workers for the picnic. I would be responsible for the adult and children's games. I never will regret this decision, and it has paid off in so many ways.

I was going through a box in my attic, and after opening it up to my surprise here was potato sacks used long ago at a company picnic. It brought back a lot of found memories at Lockheed Martin. I kept the potato sacks at home in the attic. Long ago the sacks were used in a sack race in many company picnics.

I was finally able to take a vacation, and I was happy for it. Spring had finally come and I was ready to join up with my church singles for a retreat at Laity Lodge. This lodge was located close to Kerrville Texas in the Texas Hill Country. This Center offers a variety of retreats featuring speakers, musicians and artists of the highest quality from around the country. The singles at the First Methodist Church of Clear Lake, Texas have used this Retreat Center now for many years. The Center covers 1900 acres of pristine Hill Country, Laity Lodge provides a unique blending of faith and nature experienced through the immense beauty of the Frio Canyon in Central Texas.

A myriad of outdoor activities including hiking, swimming, tennis, and cannoning will guarantee that you'll never forget your visit. This unique Center is owned by H. E. Butt Corporation. This would be my first visit. Our group on the way to Laity Lodge would stop for Mexican food at San Antonia, Tex. This is a welcome break and the food is supper. We had rented a van with ten singles from our church and headed for Laity Lodge. We were excited on this adventure because some of us were selected to play a part in providing teaching, music, and singing for the entire singles at the Lodge. I and seven others were chosen to entertain everyone in the morning and in the evening. When we are finished in the evening we all hold hands in unity in a circle to praise our Lord. But on the last night, I asked the cooks and others cleaning up the Mess Hall, if they would join us and they were happy to be included. So we all, hand in hand were unified that night. This is a standard ritual now at the Lodge. As the Frio River follows through the canyon one can swim or just get a suntan. I found out that most girls preferred to get a lot of sun, and allowed me to put a lot of sun location onto their backs, what a way to introduce myself.

There were cabins to stay for a weekend that were located far back into the woods. The people that rent the cabins are those that need solitude and peace of mind. There is a large ledger in each cabin that one can put into writing, what peace means to this person. I visited one of the cabins and read through all of the beautiful words expressing their selves in the ledger. I was amazed at the people, what peace of mind they projected within their ledgers. A lot of poets have spoken about being along, but not along. People need to take stock of where they want to end up and not hurry through life. On my next trip to Laity Lodge, I plan on going to one of the cabins and read more about the people who stayed and put their expression of peace in one of the ledgers.

Hiking is a popular thing people do at the lodge; Ann Matthews, a lovely lady that I had met at the retreat, she and I found carvings on large oak trees that were put there many years ago. People left their mark while visiting this beautiful land. We found a heart shaped carving with unknown names carved; surely love is still present at this site.

The next morning after tuning our guitars we began with an introduction to a new song. The title of the song was "HOPE". We asked the singles to stand, and then we sang the lyrics for this song. Everyone, knowing that this was the end of the singles retreat, sang with all with their hearts. This was a positive song, an inspiration to all. Some of the singles had been rejected by someone and were still hurting. The words were up lifting and each single was validated this morning. Now it was time to say till we meet again. Every single left with a full hear. The next morning as we were leaving the lodge, our group came upon the Frio River with all the other groups. An old saying that goes like this, "just pour your self out into this river, and all of your troubles will be carried down the river for healing." I along with each single man and women did just that. Three other churches had sent their singles to spend time at Laity Lodge. I truly believe that the majority of all were impressed by the Love and Hope they were given on our journey of faith. I needed this vacation to set my mind and heart straight. I will go home now with a glad heart.

I was assigned work for the up-coming launch of Apollo 15. My team was to evaluate the safety for all the extra-vehicular activity (EVA) for the Astronauts. Lockheed was assigned this job for safety procedures. I was happy to be picked and joined a team of Professional Engineers. Apollo 15 was the ninth manned mission in the Apollo Program, the fourth to land on the Moon, and the eighth successful manned mission. It was the first of the "J Missions", long stays on the Moon, with a greater focus on science than had been possible on previous missions. It was also the first mission on which the

Lunar Roving Vehicle was used. The mission began on July 26, 1971, and ended on August 7. At the time **NASA** called it the most successful manned flight ever achieved. Commander David Scott and Lunar Module Pilot James Irwin spent three days on the Moon, including 18.5 hours outside the spacecraft on Lunar EVA. At the same time, Command Module Pilot Alfred Worden orbited the Moon, using a Scientific Instrument Module (SIM) in the Service Module (SM) to study the lunar surface and environment in great detail with a panoramic camera. The lunar rover made it possible to extend the range of the astronauts on the Moon. With 173 pounds of moon rocks, including one the prize artifacts of the Apollo Program, a sample of ancient lunar crust called the "Genesis Rock." With my team working to evaluate the safety of the Mission, we had played a part in this **NASA** success story.

With a holiday coming up I wanted to see Ann Matthews who lived in Kerrville Texas, who attended Laity Lodge with me. I was up early on Saturday morning ready to hit the road and start my trip to see her. She had invited me to stay with john and his wife, a good friend of heir's while I was in town. Ann was already planning a party at her house and I was invited. She was glad that I had come to spend time with her. The trip went well for me as I pulled into the driveway of Ann's home. What a greeting, the two of us were glad to be together again. The next day Ann wanted to show me around town. I truly was taken on a grand tour, we hade dinner at a café that was steeped in history. Late that evening I went back to John's home still thinking of how beautiful Ann was, this was inward beauty. The next day we all went to the church of John and his wife, after the service we went to Ann Matthews home for her party. Ann had the party catered, the house was all decorated and the smell of the food was inviting. Ann had saved a space for me next to her at the table. After ever one had left the party, Ann and I said till we meet again and I left with a song in my heart.

I made it home safe, I had to keep my mind on the business at hand, the mission of Apollo 16. President Nixon was deeply affected by the near tragic events of Apollo 13. He felt very connected to the crew during their ordeal. As a result, Nixon proposed to cancel Apollo 16 and 17 ahead of the 1972 election, for fear that something could go wrong with one of the missions and impact his re-election bid.

The next mission was Apollo 16, scheduled for launch on April 1972. It could take a year or more for the Astronauts to train for a mission, but all was looking good for this mission. Overtime had started and our engineering team was supporting the **NASA** Safety Center, for Mission Assurance. Their motto, is it Safe, If not then make it safe. The Astronauts on this mission were John Young, Commander, with Charles Duke as Lunar Module Pilot and Thomas Mattingly II. As Commander Module Pilot. This was the fifth American landing on the Moon. My team worked with all three astronauts for safety training for their mission on the lunar surface and for water egress safety training. I was impressed with John Young because of his dedication to what was needed on any mission. His strong engineering skills where admired by his fellow astronauts. He was always asking questions for how he could improve safety and get the job done. Astronauts were fathers, friends, and caring people who respected others in their field of expertise at **NASA**. John Young was ready to work alone side others to achieve the goals of the mission. John Young lived in EL Largo, near Clear Lake, Tex. I was proud to have worked with this great man as well as all the other astronauts. John Young would eventually become Chief of the Space Shuttle Branch of the Astronaut Office at Johnson Space Center in 1973.

The astronauts for Apollo 16 went to several training locations within the U.S. that had a rocky surface and the desert to prepare for their mission. Their selections were to simulate the rough surface of the Moon. They traveled to Nevada for the desert terrain, to simulate the arid conditions on the Moon. This would help by utilizing the Lunar Rover on the Moon and moving around to explore the surface. Their locations were kept secret because of the press and with people interfering with their training. The Apollo spacecraft were designed to return to Earth by landing in the ocean, which meant extensive water egress training for the astronauts. This involved practicing with a model spacecraft at **NASA** Training Pools and in the Gulf of Mexico. This was for emergency purposes to climb out of the spacecraft and then get into a life raft until the Coast Guard helicopter would arrive to save them. Our team of Engineers working for The **NASA** Safety Center would document the Apollo egress safety training for the Astronauts.

The first objective of this mission was to investigate the lunar surface of the Moon around the Descartes area. To have the lunar rover travel southwest to Flag Crater for sample collection, later to go south to the Spook Crater, and back by the lunar module. All together this objective lasted almost 7 hours. The second objective was to start with a drive south to Stone Mountain, where surface and core samples where collected at two stations in the Cinco Craters area. Then using the lunar rover, the crew drove north to North Ray Crater to collect samples inside the crater rim. Heading south, the crew stopped at Shadow Rock for more samples and taking a lot of pictures. Then the crew was ready for the lunar Module and home. The Lunar Rover was so important for this mission to cover the distance from place to place and retain sampling. All together the crew driving around the lunar surface of the Moon was 14 hours and 23 minutes. This was another "J Missions" Long Stays on the Moon.

Let me explain just how much fun the Astronauts had while on the Moon. They put the Lunar Rover to an evaluation of strength, agility, and power. The crew put the lunar rover through a "Grand Pix" exercise consisting of S-turns, hairpins turns, and hard stops was also to be conducted. So the crew of Apollo 16 was having a lot of fun at the same time they accomplished their mission. The Lunar Rover stood up to every test they through at it, thus proving the lunar rover was safe to use. One cannot forget as they recall their own fun activities while on the Moon after returning to Earth. Talking about recall, I am taken back to my boy hood day's looking up at the Moon and wondering if man will ever walk on its surface. My Space Journey has taken me so far, and I am very Blessed.

At this time the Astronauts were preparing for Apollo 17, this was another J-type mission, using the battery-powered Lunar Roving Vehicle, or LRV. This was the last of the Apollo Missions, as President Nixon moved to end this era of Apollo. The Space Shuttle era was born. The benefits of using the Space Shuttle was too build the International Space Station (ISS). To build a working platform in space, for the Astronauts were to work and live in a zero gravity environment. There were talks about going to Mars in the future. President Nixon had cut the **NASA** budget to 3.4 billion dollars.

For The crew of Apollo 17, Eugene A. Cernan was the Commander. Harrison H. Schmitt was Lunar Module Pilot, and Ronald E. Evans was Command Module Pilot.

The crew of Apollo 17 had rehearsed their mission many times, and used the Lunar Rover for test runs to retrieve rock and material from a Moon like area in the American desert. They had to know that this was the end of the Apollo era; they were the last of the Apollo Astronauts to go to the Moon. They did not let this interfere with the mission at hand. They were proud of being the last crew to stand on the Moon and salute the American Flag. They had to practice the egress training for splash down, many times. My team was trained to work with the astronauts for safety in a **NASA** large pool of water, to help with training of the crew. Over time the crew was certified to go to the Moon. The Astronauts were anxious to put all their training to use. They blasted off from Kennedy Space Center on December 7, 1972. The crew main objective was taking lunar surface samples at the area of Taurus- Littrow region, to deploy the Apollo Lunar Surface Experiments Package, a Lunar Seismic profiling, lunar surface gravimeter or LSG, lunar atmospheric composition experiment, and meteorites. After all of the experiments came a new one, biomedical experience included the Biostack II. The Lunar Rover assisted the crew with transporting a total of 243 pounds of samples and rocks.

A little humor after the crew landed on the Moon, Eugene Cernan had an accident with the lunar rover, after he brushed against a fender with his suit full of tools and tore almost half of it off. This was serious, because the finder was there in purpose to keep out the Moon Dust from getting on the Astronauts and equipment. Just how would someone do the repairs, well with good old American logic, Cernan found a roll of gray duct tape in his supplies. He taped on the fender several times to make the repair work. Later on, it was Harrison Schmitt turn to prove that he could carry a tune. Schmitt began to skip along the surface of the Moon while singing, "I was strolling on the Moon one day" when Cernan joined in with his rendition of The Fountain in the park but they don't agree on how to perform the next line. The two astronauts were having fun and enjoying them selves. After all this was the last mission to the Moon. This was all taped and this incredible footage will be viewed many times over. The crew returned to earth on December 19, 1972. But a lot of people were sad to see the end of the Apollo era. Many managers had said that Apollo 18-20 was planned, many felt betrayed because of politics in Washington.

The future of the Space Program following the cancellation of future Apollo missions was a small earth orbiting space station named Skylab. This small earth orbiting space station was launched unmanned on May 14, 1973 utilizing a modified Saturn V Rocket with a weight of 170,000 pounds. The Skylab space station was built from leftover hardware from the Apollo Missions. My team worked with **NASA** to help with the design. It was 82.4

feet in length, 55.8 feet in width, and height was 36.3 feet. This small space station was orbiting earth from 1973 to 1979. Skylab included a workshop, a solar observatory, and scientific experiments. One could say that the Solar Observatory was one the major functions of Skylab. Solor science was advanced by its telescope and its observation of the sun was unprecedented. There were a total of three manned explorations too the station, all were conducted between May 1973 and February 1974. Each of these missions delivered a three-astronaut crew, carried in the Apollo Command / Service Module (Apollo CSM) launched atop the Saturn IB rocket, which is much smaller than the Saturn V rocket. For the final two manned missions to Skylab, a backup Apollo CSM/Saturn IB was assembled and made ready in case an in-orbit rescue mission was needed, but this backup vehicle was never flown. Skylab orbital workshop is where the Astronauts worked on their experiments. At the rear of the station included a large waste tank, propellant tanks for maneuvering jets, and a heat radiator.

The Soviet Space Program with Soyuz 11 was tasked to work with Skylab, on June 7, 1971. Three Russian cosmonauts in their spacecraft Soyuz 7K-0KS docked with The Space Station. The Russian crew members were Georgy Dobrovolskt, Vladislav Volkov, and Victor Patsayev. They completed 383 Orbits in 23 days, 18 hours and 21 minutes with the crew departing on June 29. The mission ended in disaster when their crew capsule depressurized during preparations for reentry, killing the three-man crew.

BALLOONS AND COLLEGE CLASS MATES

Things were not looking good for **NASA** at this time, Budget cuts and lay-offs were commonplace now. The Air Force at this time was working with **NASA** to help each other with their Budgets. This bold endeavor to work together could save a lot of employees from layoffs.

My options were expanded in supporting **NASA** and the Air Force in their bold endeavor, due to my Secret Clearance for The Department of Defense (DOD). This gave me hope in my quest for my Faith and Space Journey. There were layoffs already due to the cancellation of the Apollo Program and thousands more to come. I was ready and able to fill a position that came to my attention. A position was posted for supporting the **NASA** Ozone Balloon flights in Palestine, Texas, I was excited and wanted to get on board. I was accepted and the following week and was assigned to the new team. We traveled to the launching site of the balloons for ozone testing. These balloons are made of 20-micron thick plastic, and are 28 million cubit feet in volume when fully inflated with helium, and 400 feet in diameter. The balloons weigh approx. 4000 pounds. The scientific Payload weights about 3,000 pounds and is six feet square by 15 feet high. The payload would separate on command and later was retrieved. The balloons were launched by the National Scientific Balloon Facility. They would now come under the control of **NASA.** They could climb up higher than the ozone belt of our planet. They were beautiful, white in color and they carried a payload with instruments to measure the ozone and other purposes. Our team was to interpret the payload instruments and give the results to **NASA**. We would go back in the evening to our Motel to have a good meal and a good rest. There were four of us in our team, all fairly young engineers and full of energy. At the Balloon Facility the crews prepared for the balloons to be inflationed and then launched. Balloons needed good weather during periods of light stratospheric winds. The tracking of the payloads by Electronic devices during and after recovery was the job of the recovery crew. I will list the types of research for which balloons are used are Cosmic Ray studies, Ozone studies, Gamma Ray and x-Ray Astronomy, Infrared Astronomy, Atmospheric Sciences, and Cosmic Microwave Background Studies.

In over 25 years of operation, the Facility has launched more than 1700 balloons for 35 universities, 23 other research agencies, and 33 foreign groups. The average payload increased from 407 pounds in 1964 to more than 3000 pounds in 1988.

Our team would head for the electronic lab for engineering support for retrieval of data from each payload. If not real busy we could watch as the balloons were launched. This was an exciting time in my life, and I learned the benefits of trying something knew and challenging. We worked at the Balloon Facility for over two months, and then we were called back to **NASA** at Johnson Space Center.

Later on in history this **NASA** Facility would play a big part in helping the debris recovery for the Space Shuttle Columbia on February 1, 2003. I will cover this tragic event later on.

On February 1, 2006, the National Scientific Balloon Facility of **NASA** was renamed the Columbia Scientific Balloon Facility. The official renaming ceremony was held at the facility on February 23, 2006.

I was happy and sad at the same time, sad that our work was over; a new engineering team would replace our team. We were headed back to Johnson

Space Center. On the way back we all stopped in Spring, Texas, at a famous café called the Whistle Stop Café. This old café was known for its location next to a railroad track. The train engineer had to blow his whistle many times at the crossing, so people in years past would get up from their table to see the train pass by. Any old train has a place in my heart, reminding me of that boy hood love for trains. Still today people enjoy this old café and the train. The most favored meal is still the Chicken fried steak and then with a slice of apple pie to finish off a fine meal.

After returning to work, my Manager called me into his office to give me the bad news, I was to be laid off—- This hit me between the eyes, I was speechless and needed answers. It was only because of the budget, He heated to tell me, and our team would be disbanded. I asked when this was final and he said soon, but you still have two weeks. I was at a very bad place at this time of my life, to be laid off so soon and I started doubting my Faith. Why has My Lord abandon me? I asked, but no answer. I felt all-alone, was my pride the problem? I remember telling my friends how lucky I had it, with so many people being laid-off, was this the end of my Space and Faith journey. I wanted to finish my journey; I had so much to give to the Space program. That evening after work I was discouraged completely upset with my self and had questions about my faith. I did not sleep well at all. I was in a crisis mode, How can I make a trip that is already planned with my college classmates. Will I appear like I had lost my self or will I get myself together? I prayed to the Lord to please give me the courage to overcome my doubts and fears.

It was a beautiful spring day and I was thinking about seeing my college classmates. Some time back we had planned a class get together in Galveston, Texas. Classmates were all scattered across Texas. My thoughts now turned to my college and my good friend and classmate Miss Shannon. That tall good-looking girl who was in my study group at college would be coming to the reunion with 15 other classmates. After returning home on Friday, I packed and was off to see everybody in Galveston. We were on a three-day adventure; a holiday really came in handy for our get together. We planned on having fun, but resting also, everyone needed to get in touch with someone in our study group. So we planned out each day to have time to our selves. There were eight girls and eight men, all were happy to get away and recall the days of our study group and our college. The girls wanted to go shopping on Saturday morning, so the guy's went on a morning fishing trip. That evening we all got back together and each one of us talked about how important our study group was for our GPA, but also for character building over a fine seafood dinner. The next day we were up early and boarded the Galveston Ferry to enjoy the ride over to see the old lighthouse. This lighthouse was full of history dating back to the Civil War. On this day all the guy's paired up with a girl, I found Shannon to be more beautiful that I could remember, we had so much to tell each other. This was a magical day, made for fun among the young. We stopped later on at a roadside café to quince our thrust and get our bearings. Later we caught the ferry and watched while we fed the seagulls circling above us. We still had time to discover other parts of the Island that we had not yet visited. This evening we would all get dressed up for a grand time at the Galvez Hotel where we were staying. This was a special time and place to enjoy each other's company. A number of classmates were returning to the Houston Airport. All came to be a part of this grand adventure of getting to see each other and to catch up on where we were heading in life. I will truly miss this group and especially my dear Shannon, like an Irish Rose, lively and gracious. Shannon could tell that something was bothering me, I finally opened-up and explained my dilemma at **NASA.** Shannon listened to me as I explained my situation in detail to her. She held my hand so tight and looked deep into my eyes. She said do not be afraid, our Lord has not and will not abandon you. I felt courage to fight the fear that had me so afraid. I held her in my arms for a long time. I saw her off at the airport and said thank you for believing in me and we parted once more. When the outlook is not good, we should not fret. We need a change of perspective to realize that **God** sees tomorrow more clearly, than we can. The future is in his hands.

I was blessed for this opportunity on my Space and Faith Journey. In time I would realize that my **Lord** has a Blessing for me, a very special one. Yes he has not abandon me.

HISTORY OF THE SPACE SHUTTLE ERA, ORBITAL SPACE SHUTTLE STS-1

It was a dream come true for so many men and women all over our nation and for those who worked at the Palmdale, California factory to build the Space Shuttle. They worked day and night shifts to finish the Space Shuttle on time. These factory workers were laid off in the past years. Thousands of people were also laid off at Johnson Space Center plus other **NASA** sites. It was years after the Apollo Program was canceled that **NASA** came back to life. Due to my experience working with **NASA** and the Air Force I was spared to peruse my Space and Faith Journey, with my faith Compass guiding me onward.

President Nixon met with **NASA** Administrator James Fletcher and Deputy Administrator George Low, to announce the Space Shuttle decision held at San Clemente California on January 5, 1972. The first fully functional Orbiter was the Columbia and designated OV-102. It was built in Palmdale California by Rockwell International and delivered to Kennedy Space Center on March 25, 1979. The STS-1 was launched on April 12, 1981 with a crew of two astronauts.

The Space Shuttle was officially called the Space Transportation System (STS). The Space Shuttle would become the workplace in space to build the International Space Station (ISS). **NASA's** budget was hurting due to a huge budget cut. At about this same time the U.S. Air Force had two of its piloted space projects were canceled. The Air Force working with the Department of Defense (DOD) and the National Reconnaissance Office (NRO) would now cooperate with **NASA** to place DOD Astronauts in Orbit.

In turn, by serving the Air Force and the Department of Defense needs. The Space Shuttle became a truly national system, carrying all military as well as civilian payloads. The Air force could now use the Shuttle to expand their satellite reconnaissance network, to use the Shuttle to launch spy satellites from the cargo bay of the Space Shuttle. This is what saved a lot of us Engineers from layoff. I was attached to the Air Force via the Department of Defense and the National Reconnaissance Office for the Space Shuttle Program, Columbia STS-1.

The first Space Shuttle to be built was named Enterprise, although it never flew in Space. It was assembled in Palmdale, California by Rockwell Corporation. The contract began in 1972, and this vehicle was to be used to test critical phases of landing and other aspects of shuttle preparations. Enterprise was given the vehicle designation of OV-101. Enterprise was rolled out September 17, 1976. This Shuttle was mounted and launched from a modified Boeing 747 Aircraft.

The first orbital spacecraft was designated STS-1 (Space Transportation System –1), began in Palmdale, California and was launched April 12, 1981. Not only was this the first manned launch of the Space Shuttle, but it marked the first time that solid –fuel rockets were used for a **NASA** manned launch. (Although all of the Mercury and Apollo Astronauts) had relied on a solid- fuel motor in their escape towers). STS-1 was also the first U.S. manned space vehicle launched without an unmanned powered test flight. The STS-1 orbiter Columbia, also holds the record for the amount of time spent in the Orbiter Processing Facility (OPF), before launch-610 days. The time needed for the replacement of many of its heat shield tiles. The Solid

Fuel Rockets were manufactured at the **NASA** Facility in New Orleans, were I had worked long ago. The memories come racing back to me. I had the best friends that one could ask for.

This was the dawn of a new space age over Cape Canaveral, just after 7am on April 12, 1981, as a fireball brighter than the Florida sun rises into a clear sky carrying the United States first reusable spacecraft. The blast -off knocks down several hundred feet of wire fence, blows apart a camera near the launch-pad, hurls away public – address speakers, and sears grass within a mile. Its rumble shakes buildings three miles away. Yet to space shuttle commander John W. Young and pilot Robert L. Crippen, the lift-off felt as smooth as glass, "It was like riding on a fast elevator". Columbia returns Americans to space after a six-year absence, exactly 20 years to the day after Soviet Cosmonaut Yuri Gagarin made man's first orbital flight. Now the Shuttle Program intends to put some 200 Americans in orbit by year 1987. But before launch, at Johnson Space Center, in Mission Control, Message to each of the Astronauts "**God Speed**" meaning "May **God** give you success on your journey" this message was given to all of the present and future crew of each Shuttle. Back then our **Lord** was held in a high position in the life and times of each Astronaut and the majority of all **NASA** employees. At times, you sometime forget how thousands of things must work together to launch the shuttle and human behavior has to play a big part.

NASA does not pay you to express anxieties and fears. Actually, the astronauts had a serious problem that second morning as well. Up in the cockpit, when we locked the faceplates onto our helmets, we could not breathe. We threw open the plates, grabbed a breath, and started looking for the problem so we would not have to scrub again. Then Loren Shriver, an astronaut in the closeout crew, found a loose connection and tightened it. The countdown continued. The crew closed the hatch, and we set there watching the dawn and the weather and reviewing all of the cue cards we have for dealing with possible problems during flight. Then I heard the three engines start up with bangs. Then the two solid – rocket boosters, there was some vibration right at first, but the shuttle kept rising and the two astronauts were thinking, **NASA** has done it. They got it all together, and hear we are.

Once we hit orbit, the astronauts were set to open the doors of the 60-foot-long payload bay. Where future flights will stow up to 32.5 tons of cargo. The huge doors would open right on cue, but they also reveal the loss of one complete thermal tile and pieces of 15 others that were insufficiently bonded to the orbiter's engine pods. Fears that critical tiles on the shuttle's bottom may also have come loose prove unfounded. Crippen said " here I am again opening the cargo bay doors" which I have done a hundred odd- times in our simulator—except this time my feet are not on the floor. Young did not get space sick as he thought he would, he spent a lot of time enjoying zero gravity. He said, "that moving around is enough". Soon I felt graceful and could fully control my body and motion. John young was the senior astronaut at **NASA**; he needed glasses to read the instrument panels. Speaking of the instrument panels, my Engineering team did extensive work on these panels. The Shuttle flight Panels must match up with the flight panels in the SAIL Facility at Johnson Space Center where I worked. The astronauts had a complex flight plan, detailing with what we were to do minute by minute. Mission Control advised us it was time to sleep. A lot of pictures were taken of the earth when we had time. On the second day, President Ronald Reagan was to give the astronauts a phone call in space, but at the time he was recovering from an assassination attempt, which had taken place two weeks before. Vice President George H.W. Bush did give the astronauts a phone call. The second day we pushed the Shuttle to accomplish tasks, everything was checked out. We felt so confident, that we asked if we could stay another day. Mission Control said no to this request, because of flight Procedure.

The primary mission objectives of the maiden flight of Columbia were to perform a general check out of the Space Shuttle system, accomplish a safe ascent into orbit and to return to Earth for a safe landing. The first payload carried on this mission was a Development Flight Instrumentation (DFI) package, which contained sensors to measuring Orbiters performance. The Orbiter's performance and the stresses that occurred during launch, ascent, and orbital flight, decent and landing. All of the objectives were met and the orbiter's space worthiness was verified.

The astronauts were given special space suits or Extravehicular Mobility Units (EMU'S) for both Young and Crippen in the event of an emergency space walk. If such an event occurred, Crippen would go outside the orbiter with Young standing by in case Crippen needed help.

After the shuttle was now heading for home her nose was pointed 40 degrees upward, so that the heat- shielding silica tiles on Columbia's under-belly would bear the brunt of the screeching heat as it broke into the upper reaches of earth's atmosphere. So if the tiles would come off, the hot plasma could burn right threw Columbia. But **NASA** had faith in the Lockheed Contractors who manufactured the silica tiles and placed them on the Shuttle. The tiles could take 2300 F. The shuttle was now lighting up the sky around Columbia. Looking outside the window the glow was a lite red, but it turned reddish orange near the super hot nose. Before long Columbia had streaked through to the full burst of sunrise washing away the glow, as the astronauts heated to see it go.

With only one chance to land the 99-ton glider safely, Young eases the billion-dollar Columbia toward a rendezvous with the Mojave Desert floor. Swooping under the shuttle in a T-38 chase plane was fellow astronauts Jon McBride and George Nelson to inspect its tiled bottom for damage. After touching down on runway 23 at Edwards Air Force Base—54 hours, 20 minutes, and 52 seconds after leaving the launch pad in Florida. Crippen said "what a way to come to California!" And Young said, "You cannot believe what a flying machine this is."

In popular culture, the song "Countdown" by Rush, from the 1982 album Signals, was written about STS-1 and the inaugural flight of Columbia. The song was dedicated to the Astronauts Young and Crippen and to the people of **NASA**, plus all the **NASA** Contractors, working to make this launch a success.

Due to a launch pad accident that led to the deaths of three men on March 19, 1981. I think it is only right that we mention this and remember these brave men. During a countdown test for STS-1, a pure nitrogen atmosphere was introduced in the aft engine compartment of Columbia to reduce the danger of an explosion from the many other potentially gases on board the orbiter. At the conclusion of the test, launch pad workers were given clearance to return to work on the orbiter, even thought the nitrogen had not yet been purged due to a recent procedure change. Three technicians, John Bjornstand, Forrest Cole, and Nick Mullon, entered the compartment without air packs, unaware of the danger since nitrogen gas is odorless and colorless, and lost consciousnesses due to the lack of oxygen. Several minutes later, another worker saw them and tried to help, but passed out himself. Finally a security guard entered the compartment with an air pack and removed the four men. These were the first launch pad deaths at Canaveral since the Apollo 1 fire, which claimed the lives of three brave Astronauts. These **NASA** employees who perished, believed in the space program and what it meant to them. **NASA** was held responsible for the death of the three Technicians and did what was honorable, as they had done in the past for the three Astronauts in Apollo 1 fire.

The SAIL Facility at the Johnson Space Center supported the entire Space Shuttle program to perform integrated verification tests. It also contained Firing Room Launch Equipment identical to that used at Kennedy Space Center. Thus complete ground verification as well as countdown and abort operations can be tested and simulated. The Laboratory contains a complete avionics mock-up of a Shuttle. While only a skeleton of an orbiter, the electronics are identical in position and type to those used on the Shuttle; it is a sufficiently faithful replica that crews sometimes prefer to use to train on, rather than the training simulators for the Shuttle. First I was assigned to manage the replacement of most of the SAIL Flight Panels for the SAIL Facility. I was now in a position to lead and train a team of Engineers.

Lyndon B. Johnson Space Center has the responsibility for the research, design, development, and testing of manned Spacecraft and associated systems, development and integration for space flight activities; application of space technology, and supporting scientific engineering, and medical research. The selection and training of astronauts; and the operation of manned space flights in the Mission Control Center.

It would be seven months before another Shuttle launch was scheduled. This allowed me to start on the new mission for Columbia STS-2. For Engineering support and safety. It would be launched on launch pad 39A at Kennedy Space Center with Commander Joe H. Engle, Pilot Richard H. Tryuly and back up crewmembers, Thomas K. Mattingly, 11 and Henry W. Hartsfield, Jr.

SHUTTLE COLUMBIA STS-2: MY SPACE ODYSSEY

This flight marked the first time an orbital manned space vehicle had been re- flown with a second crew. The launch date was November 12, 1981, almost seven months from the launch of Space Shuttle STS-1 (Space Transport System). Columbia STS-2 with Commander Joe H. Engle, with Pilot Richard H. Truly and back-up crewmembers, Thomas K. Mattingly II and Henry W. Hartsfield, Jr. were eager to make this launch a success. The space shuttle STS-2 was launched on pad – 39A at Kennedy Space Center with a return landing at Edwards AFB, with a mission duration of 2 days and 6 hours.

STS-2 again carried the DFI package, as well as the Office of Space and Terrestrial Application (OSTA-1) Payload and other remote sensing instruments, mounted on a Spacelab pallet in the cargo bay. My team and I were assigned to the Spacelab Pallet for safety consideration. Other instruments to be tested were the Shuttle Imaging Radar-A (SIR-A) for the sensing of the Earths resources. The Shuttle Robotic Arm, commonly known, as Canadarm was capable of deploying and retrieving payloads weighting up to 7,260 lb, was operated successfully. The Canadarm will be used on the International Space Station (ISS). Other experiments or tests included

Shuttle Multispectral Infrared Radiometer, measurement of air pollution from satellites plus other tests.

During this mission, President Regan called the crew of STS-2 from Mission Control Center at Houston, Texas while they were in orbit. This mission was going to last five days, but was cut short when one of the three fuel cells that produce electricity and drinking water failed. The mission was shortened by two days, and the Canadarm tests was canceled, but the crew was awake during a scheduled sleep period and tested the arm anyway, working during the Loss- of – Signal (LOS) periods when they where not in contact with Mission Control. The Canadarm operated to the satisfaction of the crew. The deorbit and reentry phase of this mission differed from STS –1, in that while the first shuttle entry was known as a "middle of the road test" of the automatic guidance, the success of that mission allowed for the STS-2 crew to explore the stability margins of the vehicle's performance. Twenty –nine planned Programmed Test Inputs (PTIs) were manually flown in the Control Stick Steering (CSS) mode, with Commander Engle making use of his past experience in the X-15 hypersonic rocket powered aircraft. More than 90 percent of the mission's objectives were achieved. But STS-2 was the first Shuttle flight where O -ring, blow-by was observed, This is caused by an O-ring erosion allowing the gas to pass or blow-by the 0-ring and this would not seal the joint. After the damage to the o-ring was discovered, another O-ring was intentionally damaged to a further degree, It was then put through a flight simulator at three times flight pressure. It survived the test, and was endorsed as flight worthy. This same problem would occur on 14 more shuttle flights, before contributing to the loss of Orbiter Challenger in 1986.

The landing phase was a success; no tiles were missing and only 12 were damaged. Chase 1 crewed by astronauts "Hoot" Gibson and Kathy Sullivan escorted Columbia on final approach at Edwards Air force Base. I am thankful that my team and I played a part for the successful safety input on the Spacelab Pallet.

Now let me tell you a good story, about the Canadarm and the Canadian personnel assigned to **NASA.** They were responsible for a robotic arm that would attach to any payload in the Shuttle Payload Compartment. This was in 1980 before the launch of Shuttle STS-2.

This is a true story about an Astronaut, his ex-wife, and the Canadian Project Manager Mr. Clark, now assigned to **NASA** at Johnson Space Center for the Canadarm. I was invited to hear a **NASA** speaker on the subject of Safety Management at the Gilruth Center at Johnson Space Center. I am interested in this subject, and my job requires my utmost attention to safety. I was seated next to this gorgeous lady that had caught my attention, she could make the room light up with her smile. She was there with a female friend of hers and they were quite a pair. As I normally do, I introduced my self to this lady setting next to me, and the room did light up following her smile. We talked a little before the speaker introduced him self. After the event was over, I got the courage up to ask her if we might see each other again. She smiled and said yes, her name was Patricia.

I was invited by Patricia to attend a church service held at the Catholic Church in Clear Lake, Texas. It was at this church that I was introduced to a Mr. Clark, who was the Project Manager working at **NASA** Johnson Space Center responsible for work on the Canadarm. Mr. Clark was a true Canadian and he was proud of it. Later on Patricia and I were invited to Mr. Clarks home. The church service was up-lifting, due to the praise music. At the Clark's home I met his wife and family, they were so kind and I felt welcome. Mr. Clark talked a lot about his responsibility at **NASA** in support of the Robotic Arm. I asked a lot of questions concerning the Safety of the Robotic Arm. Our paths would cross again with the Space Shuttle STS-3 (One never knows where friendship can lead).

Patricia and I started dating; it was then that I discovered that she was divorced from an Astronaut assigned to **NASA,** Johnson Space Center. This Astronaut name was Story Musgrave. He would fly on the Shuttle as a Spacewalker. In the past he was a doctor, highly educated, and was picked by the Astronaut Office to fly on future shuttle flights. Story Musgrave flew on six Space Shuttle Missions and in 1993, he was picked as Payload Commander for Space Shuttle STS-61, for the Hubble Telescope first repair mission where he set a record for time on his Space Walk. He was a likeable sort of man; he enjoyed flying the trainer planes at Ellington Air Force Base. His favorite thing was to ride a motorcycle with his friends. He shaved his head always, for the bike helmet. We had what one would say is a professional friendship and I maintained a good friendship with his family and Patricia and I remained good friends.

I had been in my new home now for a while. I was thankful for all my friends for lending a hand in offering to help move me into my new residence in Friendswood Texas. It was a long time coming; I had been living in a one-bed room apartment located close to the exit gate of **NASA**. I was excited and had wanted a home of my own for quite a while. I would be leaving many good friends behind, but I will see a lot of my friends at work. My friends had given me a going away party. My apartment complex was full of **NASA** employees and contractors, who were always throwing a party for someone. I remember asking Shannon to attend my party at the clubhouse but she was out of town. Why I had picked Friendswood Texas to live is because a few of my good friends told me it was a good Christian community, which is very important for me to grow in my faith. In fact I knew and worked with several astronauts who lived there.

Friendswood Texas was established by Quakers in 1895, by Frank Jacob Brown and Thomas Hadley Lewis. The two Quakers were part of the Westward Movement that established a new Colony called Friendswood on the Gulf Coast of Texas. (Quakers and Friends are Synonymous) They had picked this region of Texas to live and grow their new settlement of Quakers. It was the perfect place, fresh water from three separate branches and a forest of old oaks to build homes, churches, and to grow a community. With an inlet to the Gulf of Mexico, this was useful. The Quaker homes and enterprises are mostly gone now, but one can still visit the Quaker Museum located within this city. Now this is a bedroom community with exemplary schools and is an attractive, growing and vibrant city with a population of over 30,000 residents.

With my furniture and everything else in place, I set down and thanked my **Lord** for his gift. This home has three bedrooms, two bathrooms, a good-sized living room, excellent kitchen, and a two-car garage, everything that one could ask for. This was an older home, but well taken care of. The back yard was big enough with two large raised planters for growing things. The front yard was just right for me with a large oak tree, maybe planted by a Quaker many years ago. I can remember that large oak tree hanging over my Grandmothers home in Ingleside, Texas long ago. I truly felt at home here.

It was now in October of 1981, that I planned a trip with the Methodist Church in Clear Lake Tex. The church I attended was sponsoring a trip to the piney woods located in Montgomery County at The Lodge of The Pines. This was a weekend get-away for all singles. As I drove to the Lodge of The Pines I was looking forward to seeing my old friends and hopefully make new friends. But little did I know what really lay ahead for me. I arrived Friday afternoon around four o'clock and went to the Lodge to sign in. A lot of singles had already arrived and were introducing each other. I spotted a good-looking Lady as she was signing in, asking a lot of questions about the lodge. She was about 5 ft, 7 inches in height and boy did she have a good figure. Her blonde hair and blue eyes were beautiful and she looked to be about 120 pounds in weight. You could say that I took a while sizing up this single lady, I hope it was not too obvious to the other singles. A number of singles from other churches came on this singles event. I was transfixed on this lady, she had a way about her, and one could say that she "was truly a lady." I went over to the sign in window and introduced my self. I found out what the problem was, her home church had the opening dates wrong for this Singles Conference. I spoke up for her and the mess was all cleared up to everyone's satisfaction. She was very grateful for my help, her name was Susan Stewart.

It was now getting dark and people were heading out to see the lighting of the campfire. I kept my eyes open for Susan; she had made an impression on me. The air was getting chilly and I was happy that I had dressed warm. The fire was already started and the group was getting excited. I spotted Susan as she approached me by the fire and she still looked beautiful. We all gathered around the campfire in a large circle to sing songs that brought back memories of long ago, like **Kumbaya** (oh **Lord** won't you come by here). Susan was not dressed for the occasion but she was happy to be here. As we all held hands at the end of the campfire event, to say a prayer of thankfulness for this evening and for making new friends. Susan was snuggling up to me to keep warm; I was glad that I was there for her. I offered up my jacket to her and she was very thankful. When we returned to the lodge, Susan said thank you for everything and she gave me a big hug and kissed me on the cheek. She handed me my jacket back as she went into her cabin for the night. I felt warm inside; no jacket was needed as I went to my cabin with a big smile.

The next morning after breakfast we all gathered in the large conference room, I was now looking for Susan when I spotted her coming down the hall. This was the time for the camp leaders to tell all of us what the agenda would be today. I was excited to hear that we would have a lot of fun doing the events laid out for us. After we were given a list of things to do, I asked

Susan if she wanted to pair up with me for the day and she said yes. Now we were off to have fun. We picked archery and tennis for our time to be together, and it was a beautiful day to be outdoors laughing and playing together in the sunshine. I noticed that Susan was a very good tennis player, and she was also competive. We did not do so well in archery, but we had fun together just the same. Later in the afternoon we had time to catch a cup of coffee and talk. I wanted to know about Susan and she asked a lot about me. I explained my situation with my boys and a failed marriage. Susan listened and she was not judgmental, she said that she understood. She then explained her failed Marriage and her children. I let Susan known that everything was fine with me and she was happy.

Then Susan said to me we had to hurry if we are to get ready for the evening with good music and a great speaker on single issues. I with two others would furnish the music for the closing of the night with our guitars and songs. Susan set beside me, now it was time for the speaker; he was from a church in Houston, Texas. He talked about all of the problems of being single, and how to cope with it. This speaker was invited to our home much later on. Now it was time to celebrate the night with song and music. I picked the song called "Hope" to inspire the singles assembled here. If you remember, back a ways I used this same song at a singles event in Kernville, Texas. It was a hit then and will be a hit tonight. I got up from my chair with the other two guitar players and began strumming my instrument, and then the three of us began to sing the song of HOPE. Everyone joined in to make this truly a night of "Hope".

After all of the singing was over I looked into the eyes of Susan and I just knew that the song Hope inspired her. We hugged each other and then kissed each other, a kiss that we both felt in our hearts. It was time to say good night to Susan. On Sunday morning we would be leaving after breakfast.

Come Monday morning I would be busy with my Engineering and Safety Team. We would work on the up-coming Shuttle STS-2. As a team leader, I was picked to travel to Kennedy Space Center for Safety Engineering on the up-coming flight of Space Shuttle Columbia.

At this time there was a musical celebration for **NASA,** in the Clear Lake Community. This time they picked John Denver who could sing about his beloved Colorado. I must ask Susan to come with me.

STS-3 AND MY WEDDING DAY

Space Shuttle STS-3, was the third flight of Columbia it was launched at Kennedy Space Center on March 22, 1982, with Commander Jack R. Lousma and pilot Gordon Fullerton. STS-3 had a successful landing at White Sands NM on runway number 17. The Duration of the flight was 8 days. The mission involved extensive orbital endurance testing of the STS-3, as well as numerous scientific experiments. This was the first shuttle launch with an unpainted external tank, and the only mission to land at the White Sands Space Harbor near Las Cruces, New Mexico. This was a forced landing due to flooding at the originally planned landing site, Edwards Air Force Base.

Commander Lousma had flown as pilot of the second Skylab crew, staying aboard the space station for 59 days from July to September 1973. Lousma also served on the support crews for Apollo 9, 10, and 13. Fullerton was a rookie who transferred to **NASA** in 1969 after the cancellation of the Air Force's Manned Orbiting Laboratory Program. He had previous experience with the Shuttle when he flew the Shuttle Enterprise as a pilot alongside Fred Haise during the Approach and Landing Tests Program in 1977.

The primary objective of this flight was to continue testing the Canadarm, the Remote Manipulator System (RMS). The Canadarm was capable of deploying and retrieving payloads. Its first operational use was on this STS-3 mission to deploy and maneuver the Plasma Diagnostics Package.

In the previous chapter, I explained how friendship could lead to unexpected gifts. In my case meeting Mr. Clark was a blessing to me. We met by accident one day at **NASA** and we renewed our friendship. Mr. Clark asked me if I would like to do a safety assessment for the Canadarm on the up-coming mission of STS-3. My Manager was happy to oblige me. Mr. Clark and I met at the Training Facility for the Canadarm at Johnson Space Center to discuss the details. The Canadarm was used to retrieve, repair and deploy satellites for up-coming missions. The original Canadarm could lift items of 733 lbs. Later in the mid-1990s the arm control system was redesigned to lift 7,260 lbs for the Space Station. The arm operators see what they are doing by looking at the Advanced Space Vision Screen next to the controllers. Space Crew members train for the Canadarm in the Training Facility at **NASA** Johnson Space Center.

Another important job was to carry out extensive thermal testing of Columbia by exposing its' tail, nose, and top to the Sun for varying periods of time. This shuttle carried the DFI package and the OSS-1, which consisted of a number of instruments mounted on a Skylab pallet in its payload bay. All of the objectives of this flight were met.

I was selected for Payload Safety and for the Canadarm (RMS) for this Shuttle STS-3

For the first time, a number of experiments were stored in the shuttle's mid-deck lockers. These included an Electrophoresis Equipment Verification Test (EEVT) to study the separation of biological components, and a Mono- Disperse Latex Reactor Experiment. This was the first Shuttle for a Student Involvement Project (SSIP) – a study of insect motion carried in a mid –deck locker. High School students in the surrounding area were to compete for their Student (SSIP). I was involved with this program as a volunteer to help local high schools work toward their Student Involvement Projects. I was to make sure that the students were following the design parameters set by **NASA**. These included size, weight, and the material used, plus others. One has to figure in these items for all of the Space Shuttle Systems. First it must fit into a required space, all weight is very important for the Shuttle lift- off, and material used must pass tests for flammability and other safety tests. I enjoyed working with these students, it helped me to work closely with these bright an up-coming students. One day these students could work at **NASA.**

A variety of minor problems were experienced on this flight. First the orbiter's toilet malfunctioned on the first day of use, resulting in, according to Lousma "eight days of colorful flushing." one Auxiliary Power Unit (APU) overheated, but worked properly during descent. Both crewmembers experienced some space sickness. High winds at the White Sands Harbor reduced the visibility and delayed the landing by a day.

This was fine for the Astronauts; Lousma described this as "an extra day in our world's favorite vacation spot."

This was one of the most dramatic landings in the history of the Shuttle. The Early automatic speed brake closure had resulted in high speed on the inner glide slope and Lousma opted to touch down fast rather than excessively long. This decision saved the Shuttle by doing so. The unexpected hard landing caused the shuttle to be damaged, and required extensive repair at Kennedy Space Center. This time their escorting T-38 planes were led by Chase 1 crewed by astronaut Dick Covey and **NASA** photographer Pete Stanley.

The **NASA** wake up calls to the astronauts was a tradition of playing music was first used to wake up a flight crew during Apollo 15. The music is specially chosen, often by the astronauts' family, and has a special meaning to an individual member of the crew. On day 7, their wake up call was "This is My Country".

It was time to welcome my friends into my new home for a party. I had joined the Methodist Church in Clear Lake Texas, to have a church membership. An Astronaut friend of mine who lives in Clear Lake Tex. asked if I wanted to have my home blessed by an Elder in this church. I was thankful for this gift, and I replied yes. I knew not everyone could fit into my home that I wanted to invite. With the possibility of some not being able to come, I finally came up with a number. I invited all who helped move me into my new house and then I asked all the rest that I truly cared about. Jane Morgan came along with her husband. Jane and I worked together on a project of Total Quality Management (TQM). It made a world of difference to employees in their day-to-day function. This TQM Project also gave me another boost within the Company. I did not forget to ask my dear friend Susan Stewart from The Woodlands, Texas. First my house had a Blessing, we all held hands as we blessed my new home. Now let the party began, with friends enjoying each other's company. Someone brought a lot of games in case we got bored. Several women were serving up excellent food and drink. Everyone really had a good time and I was so happy to see my friends enjoying themselves. The party lasted well into the night and everyone felt blessed.

Later Susan and I said good night, there was an attraction on my part. I liked her personality, her smile, and her faith. Susan had a long drive home, and we set a date when we would meet again. She was winning my heart, and I knew it. I have been a single person for too long. Susan worked for a Company in The Woodlands, Texas. She was a Legal Sectary, and excellent at what she does. Mr. George Mitchell her Boss, was the founder of his Company developed The Woodlands; Texas to become home for many residents in this master planned residential community.

The next time Susan and I met was a week later to attend a Tribute to NASA, with John Denver. It was held at the Gilruth Center at Johnson

Space Center. John Denver was my favorite singer/entertainer and I was excited. Now John Denver was a big supporter of **NASA**, his interest was so great that he passed **NASA's** examination, to determine mental and physical fitness for Space Travel. He wanted to go to Space as a civilian to write a song in Space, but he never made the trip. John Denver and Bob Hope gave another tribute to **NASA**. John Denver sang a song he composed titled "High Flight" this was a song from his heart about **NASA** in Space. John Denver received the **NASA** Public Service Award Medal in 1983. He received this medal for helping to increase awareness of **NASA** Space Exploration.

Susan and I would now meet every week if we could to enjoy each other's company. She was a happy person, one who was strong in her faith. I admired her for her steadfast love of her family and friends. I would travel to The Woodlands to see her mingle with her friends; this allowed me a window into her life. I knew that this was the woman that I had been seeking for such a long time. I asked my dear friend Shannon to meet with me; I wanted to get her opinion on Susan. Shannon was a true friend and we could discuss this matter in the full light of day. Shannon had leveled with me several times back; she knew me very well. She had met a man whom she was crazy about. I was excited for her, she was extremely happy. Shannon was joyful for me also and encouraged be to go with my heart. She said that the HEART knows, trust the heart. I was ready to get married, I was mature and when I make a commitment of this magnitude I stay committed for life.

On this beautiful day, Susan and I enjoyed visiting the ice-skating rink in the Woodlands, Texas. A lot of people are not aware that The Woodlands had a very nice ice-skating rink during this time. We enjoyed our lunch at the Woodlands Country Club then we were off to see other attractions. I was blown away by the wildflowers planted in the mediums of the village roads. President Johnson's wife, Lady Bird Johnson was truly responsible for the wildflower Organization. Weeks later Susan and I while in The Woodlands were able to attend a Tribute to Mr. George Mitchell held at the Grogans Mill Village. This was the first Village in The Woodlands, Texas, but it was not the last. Susan introduced me to Mr. George Mitchell and his wife. I was totally impressed, with the quality of these two beautiful people. As time went on I was ready to ask Susan for her hand in marriage. Susan and I had talked all about our children. Susan had a young son living at home. I had three young sons living with their mother. We would have my boy's over to visit several times a month. The next time we met, I just knew that Susan would be willing to marry me. We were engaged at last and we began to plan our wedding day.

Susan wanted to get married in the Presbyterian Church of The Woodlands, Texas. This was Susan's home church and it meant a lot to her. I can remember our wedding as it was yesterday.

Chapter 8

MY WEDDING DAY

Susan and I were married on a spring day in 1982. I felt a deep sense of joy and admiration for Susan and she felt the same for me. Susan and I both went through counseling at the Presbyterian Church in The Woodlands, Texas. The counseling did help answer many questions that each of us had, like where should we live after marriage. We both owned a home; also there was a concern about Susan maintaining her current job. I was the one to step up to the plate for the concerns at hand. I knew my dear Susan loved The Woodlands and her home church. I made the sacrifice to sell my home, move to The Woodlands and commute almost 170 miles round trip to **NASA** each day. Susan was grateful but concerned that I could have an accident or worse, get injured in a car wreck. I went with faith in my decision with my **Lord** and it turned out well for us. This is not to say that I never had a car accident or a flat tire in my travels to **NASA** because I did. I found my favorite Christian music channel at 105 FM; the music was filled with **Gods** promise of hope and protection. As I listened, I sang along with the music and felt the hand of **God** on my steering wheel.

My decision to move to the Woodlands, Texas was also helped by the fact, that I enjoyed conversing with the locals. Here I found a community made up mostly by people working in the Oil and Gas industry. I was from **NASA** and the Aerospace industry. I decided it would be stimulating to live in a new environment. Also I was a golfer, here I found the best golf courses to play a game of golf. I could share my knowledge of Space with newfound friends. Susan had many close lady friends to help her arrange our wedding. Susan and I wanted a good Christian wedding that included all the things that were important to us. One thing we insisted on, was a large white candle, to be blessed by the pastor, and called the <u>Marriage Vow Candle</u>. This wedding Candle would be used each year to remind us to uphold our marriage Vows to each other. Susan and I dearly loved each other and our love build on trust grew, as we let the **Lord** lead us.

The time was growing close for the wedding and my friend Miss Karen would play the organ as a gift. The bride's maids had been chosen along with my best Man, Gordon Kemp. My parents were able to come with my Sister Jo Ann, and her daughter Kim. Susan's Parents were able to come. Susan and I had invited so many Family and friends, that we were worried about the church having enough room us for all.

The Wedding cake I remember it very well, Susan and I shopped for a cake that suited our taste and one that was well designed with three layers.

Susan and I were married in a beautiful candlelit ceremony in her home church; I remember the wedding like it was yesterday. My friend Karen played the organ as I watched my sweet hart come down the isle with her father.

I remember the placing of rings on each other's finger, the Vows we gave for each other In this church, and the love we felt was everlasting. After the wedding everybody was invited to a reception at the home of the Mathews family. This was a home situated close to the Woodlands Country Club, a large two-story home that had a large front porch.

The punch bowl was always being filled, as people kept coming into the home. Three lovely women from Susan's home church had prepared the music for this celebration. The music was up lifting and beautiful because, this was a gift to Susan and I. One dear lady friend of Susan's had written the words to a song that she and two other ladies sang, while playing their guitars. Susan and I felt so special to have such loving friends at this time in our life.

I will never forget my wedding day; it was one of the happiest moments of my life. It was time to thank everyone who came, and one last hug from our family and friends, as we headed out for our honeymoon.

After coming home from our honeymoon, we were ready to start our life together in The Woodlands, Texas. Both of us were still working, Susan in the Woodlands and I was supporting **NASA**. The following week-end I was up at 6AM on this Saturday morning, to head out for my bike ride. This would turn out to be a joyous time with my **Lord**. The Woodlands is a beautiful place, where one can get close to our Lord, in the nature of his love. I was becoming aware of his present with me. At this moment in life, I become Joyous, reaching out to my **Lord** with praise, thankfulness, and love for leading my wife to me. This was **God's** answer to a new life shared by two, with love and respect for each other.

With joy in my heart, I felt assured that my Sons, Bryan, Craig, and Christopher, would now have a loving home to visit in The Woodlands with Dad, Susan, and her Son Jeff. I would raise her son as my own, with love and caring. All of the son's would be loved and treated equally. When my three boys came over to visit on a weekend in the summer, there was always fun to be had. There was swimming in our large pool, eating out, visiting the maul, taking long nature hikes, bike riding, and Church. There were many happy memories to be made by all.

COLUMBIA STS-4 WITH TQM PROGRAM

Space Shuttle, STS-4 was launched from Kennedy Space Center (KSC) on the 27th of June 1982. The crewmembers were Ken Mattingly as commander, and Henry Hartsfield as pilot. This Shuttle flight was the last research and development flight in the program. NASA considered the Shuttle now operational. After this flight, Columbia's ejection seats were deactivated and shuttle crews would not wear pressure suits again until STS-26 in 1988. I was assigned for Payload Safety and Mission Assurance on this Shuttle Mission.

The STS-4 cargo consisted of the first Getaway Special Payloads, including nine scientific experiments provided by students from Utah State University. The Getaway Special was a **NASA** program that offered individuals or groups; opportunities to fly small experiments aboard the Space Shuttle. Over the 20- year history of this program, over 170 missions were flown.

The Shuttle carried the classified US Air Force Payload of two missile- launch detection systems that failed to operate. In the shuttles mid-deck, a Continuous Flow Electrophoresis System and the Mono-disperse Latex Reactor flew for the second time. The crew conducted a test with the hand-held cameras and performed medical experiments on each other. They operated the Remote Manipulator System with an instrument attached. It was called the Induced Environment Contamination Monitor, designed to obtain information on particles being released by the Shuttle orbiter in flight.

Columbia STS-4 landed on 4 July at 9:09 am, on the runway at Edwards Air Force Base. President Ronald Regan with his wife Nancy would welcome the crew upon arrival. Following the landing The President gave a speech to the crowd gathered at Edwards, during which he declared the Space Shuttle operational. He was followed by remarks from Mattingly and Hartsfield and a flyover of the new Shuttle Challenger headed for Kennedy Space Center. The STS-4 achieved all the objectives. The wake-up-call on day 3 was "Hold That Tiger".

I would get up at 5 AM every morning to get myself ready; first I have my coffee, later I pull the old Bible out to read. I promised the **Lord** that I would read the bible from cover to cover. This is a promise made and a promise kept over the years, I read for about ten minutes, and then I say a prayer for my safe return. Susan is now up to fix me breakfast and talk about my drive to work, as she hands me my coffee on my way out. I know that my wife will be praying for my safe return. I will now leave to begin the long hard drive to **NASA.**

I always set my radio to FM 105, a radio station in Houston Texas that plays a good variety of Christian Music. In the morning the station will play the most inspirational music. It has sustained me over the years. I still fell the hand of **God** on my steering wheel.

I have truly married a good and understanding wife. Before we were married, she and I talked about my schedule at work, and I knew what her schedule was. The two of us knew each other well, when I had to work over time, she understood. Especially when I had to take a management class and stayed late. I would arrive at home around eleven o'clock at night. My sweetheart would have my supper warmed and ready, and a kiss to welcome me home, what more can a man ask for. Susan continued to work as a legal sectary at Mitchell Corp. She and I were blessed to enjoy our life together. We were a family now and enjoying all that The Woodlands, Texas has to offer. This was a planned community with the most churches one can find. We would go to the Community Presbyterian Church of The Woodlands, Texas each Sunday with our family. The family consisted of Susan's son Jeff and my three sons. Later on, Bryan my eldest son would start staying at home, this left my two younger sons to visit on the weekends. With Jeff and my two sons Chris and Craig, we were a family and soon the three boys were called "The Three Musketeer's"

In 1983, Management was ready for a Total Quality Management Program (TQMP) to improve the quality of work. Lockheed wanted me to lead and manage a team for this purpose. Lockheed was expanding into Quality Circles, this was for all the employees. This program would empower each employee to advance the quality of things produced. Quality Circles were a big part of TQMP. My team and I worked to achieve our Company's Total Quality Management Program. Everyone on the team received a commendation for their work. Later on in 1989, the TQMP would be a part of the **NASA** Excellent Award for all of Lockheed Employees.

Chapter 10

COLUMBIA STS –5 WITH FOUNDATIONS

Columbia STS-5 was launched on November 11, 1982 from Kennedy Space Center. STS-5 returned to land at Edwards Air Force Base on November 16 on runway 22. The four-crew members on this Shuttle are Commander Vance D, Brand, Pilot Robert F. Overmyer, Mission Specialist 1, Joseph P. Allen, and Mission Specialist 2, William B. Lenoir.

This was Columbia's first time to use 4 crewmembers, and the first mission to deploy two communication satellites into orbit. The two satellites were the SBS-3 owned by Satellite Business Systems, and the Anik C3, owned by Telesat Canada. Hughes Corp.

This shuttle also carried a West German- sponsored micro gravity GAS experiment canister in the payload bay. The crew conducted three student –designed experiments.

The two communication satellites were deployed successfully and where propelled into their operational geosynchronous orbits by McDonnell Douglas PAM-D kickmoters. Just prior to release, the satellite was spun on a turntable to a speed of 50 revolutions per minute. At the right moment, following precise alignment of Columbia, the satellites was spring -ejected from the cargo bay. The satellite drifted away from the shuttle at a speed of approximately one meter per second. The crew of the spacecraft maneuvered into a new orbit and receded to a safe distance. At this time, a rocket booster attached to the satellite sent SBS –3 into a highly elliptical transfer orbit. Later when the satellite reached the peak altitude, after several orbits of earth, a small rocket fired and changed the orbit shape to a circle. SBS-3 was now in a geosynchronous orbit above earth. The next day the satellite ANIK –C-3 was launched in the same manner.

Astronauts Lenoir and Allen were to do a planned space walk; they were Space Walkers and were looking forward to their adventure. This was the first for the space shuttle program. The space walk was postponed by one day after Lenoir become ill, and then they cancelled the space walk when their spacesuits developed problems.

This was the first Shuttle flight in which the crew did not wear pressure suits for the launch and return flight. They choose for their wake up call on day 3 "Cotton Eye Joe."

I was blessed with having the responsibility for leading the team for Payload safety and Mission Assurance for Columbia STS-5. Joseph Allen and I were good friends; he will be a Spacewalker on other Space Shuttle Missions.

I will now tell you about my journey for the organization of a Mentorship Program that I was responsible for at Lockheed Corp. and **NASA**. It all began one morning when my Manager asked me to lead a team for a Mentorship Program for Lockheed Martin. I was surprised and humbled at the same time. He explained to me about the need for a Mentoring Program with in our company and he thought I should lead this effort.

A Mentorship Program needs to utilize these six things: a sponsor, a guide, a coach, a companion, one who plants seeds, and a demonstrator.

We need mentors in our lives, a person that sees something of value or worth that you possess, but is hidden from you. A mentor can help you see your **God** given value, to help you live out you life's journey. I have always been blessed with a mentor in my life.

I began my Journey long ago with my parents as "<u>Coach Mentors</u>", and my English Teacher in High School, Mrs. Shelton as "<u>one who plants seeds</u>." and my football coach as "<u>a Demonstrator</u>" I have been blessed so many times when someone has agreed to be a mentor for me, in my journey of space and faith.

One must mirror oneself thru others vision, of what they see in you. And <u>show respect</u> for a mentor, because this person works to help you be all that you can be. This is their calling to help you believe in yourself and accomplish your goals.

First I looked high and low for a viable mentoring program that is being used in the NASA area. One must always look to other leaders who have put a mentoring program in place. After much interviewing with company leaders I finally found the perfect leader, a Miss Jeannie Kranz from Rockwell Corp. She had already formed a Mentoring Program called "Foundations-Building Upon the Past." She was more than willing to help me in any way she could. Miss Kranz and I became dear friends. She also kept me informed on her progress, and said that I could use her mentoring program to get me started.

I chose to use "Foundations" as my guiding light with my Company. This is what the foundations of an institution has with provisions for future maintenance. That's exactly what the Founders of the Space Program did. A pilot program with mentors can be initially for the class of new employees of their company. This is needed to give new employees an opportunity to be mentored, and learn about the company, its goals and each other, and to learn about people who have made significant contributions to the Space Program past and present.

The program appropriately named "Foundations", also provides the opportunity to network among individuals from the same organization. To discuss the challenges in the future, the obstacles, the successes and the defeats, stimulate new ideas and to discuss any issues within our Space Environment.

I first thought about the new employees coming to work for Lockheed and what did they need most to succeed in life. The answer was Mentoring.

The first thing was to form a team of a unified group of employees that began to plan a Mentorship Program called "Foundations." I was to help plan and facilitate this group. We would work with Company Leaders to put a Mentorship Program in place. All were in agreement to place new employees under a trained mentor, and then seasoned employees next. With the help of trained mentors in place, new employees could receive the help and guidance they need. The second stage was to use mentors to up-date seasoned employees.

I am happy to say that this group worked well together and finished proud and on time. Lockheed Corp. was pleased with our work. Soon the Mentorship Program was put in place. Mentors were sought out and trained to help their employees in their Company Divisions. Our team received praise and Commendations for our effort to create this Mentoring Program called "Foundations." As the Leader responsible for this team effort, I will be ever grateful for each team member and for all their sacrifice to get the job done. I invited my manager and mentor, Mr. Christopher C. Kraft, to give a talk for our new Lockheed Mentoring Group. He spoke about the need for this program called Foundations, Mr. Kraft, "You must be the leaders" was the title of his speech.

NASA now saw the value of having a Mentorship Program like "Foundations." My company was happy to help out. Lockheed Martin asked me to work with **NASA** officials to achieve a new Mentorship Program of their own. Now employees at **NASA** Sites through out the USA will be helped through this Mentorship Program. I consider this is one of my major achievements of my career, made possible by all of my Mentors who saw the **God-Given** Value in me.

PACER COIN PROJECT

I was at work, when my Project Manager called me into his office; he said that he had put my name on a list to be saved from this layoff. I could not believe what I was hearing, he said that Mr. Jacobs, a Project Manager remembered my name and wanted me to work for him on a new assignment called Pacer Coin for The Air force. A while back I covered how we are known by our Name, each of us leave foot prints that define us. I remember meeting Mr. Jacobs at the company picnic; he had also volunteered to work this day. After the picnic was over we had a discussion about serving the Company with pride. He never did forget my name. When you have a sense of yourself and what you're her to do, that's leadership. Mr. Jacobs could not express the importance of the Pacer Coin Project to the USA. Mr. Jacobs knew me well, and with his assurance, that I would be an asset to the Pacer Coin team, I accepted this task that lay ahead of me.

The next morning as I was heading for work, I was thinking about my new job and what was expected of me. All I knew is what my new Manager had stated that it was urgent that I start on a new assessment called The Pacer Coin Project for the Air force in Ontario California. This was a little unusual and puzzling at the same time. I was called to support the Department of Defense (DOD) for the Air Force. I knew that this was Top Secret, so I can only tell what is now unclassified knowledge. I was chosen because I held a Top Secret Clearance, I was qualified, and I could lead a team of Engineers. I was to go with two other engineers and help get the project off and running. The time it would take would depend on the progress of the Air Force who was in control. I was thankful for this project, the Space Shuttle would take a few years to build and time for testing. Without the Pacer Coin Project, I would be unemployed and my dreams to be put on hold, so I was truly blessed.

Susan and I had only been married for a short while and she was a little up-set, but she understood. I did not want to leave her either, but I knew the **Lord** had a part in all of this. We would make things work out for us. We would communicate by writing a lot of letters and by phone calls.

We finally arrived at the airport in Ontario, California. This was a fine fall day and our lodging was at the Best Western Hotel, which had everything one could ask for. We talked about the work we had to do at this Lockheed Facility over dinner. I was excited to learn that my good friend Mr. Rey Rivas who was in charge of this mission. We had worked together before, so I knew that I was in good hands when he had asked for me. The other engineer was named Mike. The next morning we arrived at the Lockheed facility, was signed it with the Security Personnel. Then we meet the Lockheed Manager over the Pacer Coin Project. Mr. Wilson who was a straight talking mature manager. He welcomed each of us and was glad that we had the time to come down and start on the project so soon. Mr. Wilson and I hit it off great because I had learned to respect his age and all that he had accomplished while working as an Engineering Manager at this Lockheed Facility. Later on when the too of us were along, he confided in me, that he would be retiring soon, I wished the very best for him and his family. As we talked, he gave me a friend's name that worked as a lead Engineer for Lockheed and the Air force. This was what I was looking for, some one that knew the system of the Air force C130 -Pacer Coin Project. I had a new friend to help guide me through this entire Project.

Pacer Coin is a daytime, all-weather reconnaissance and surveillance system, which provides imagery intelligence support.

Pacer Coin in the future would be used to support Special Operations Forces and The United States Counter-drug operations in the Western Hemisphere. Pacer Coin and Flowing Pen are two C-130 aircraft operations, which deploy to Howard AFB six times a year for a two-week period. The Pacer Coin mission is flown by the Nevada Air National Force and is a vital information gathering resource for SOUTHCOM'S counter drug efforts.

The Pacer Coin Mission transitioned to the Air National Guard, and the 152nd Air Wing in Reno, Nevada. The Nevada National Guard is also transitioned to an airdrop mission, and is receiving additional C-130 Aircraft dedicated to this mission. By making the Pacer Coin Aircraft dual -use the utilization and mission capability of these aircraft will be significantly broadened. This modification will enable the Pacer Coin aircraft to maintain a primary mission of air/drop/transport, while preserving the unique imagery capabilities of the Pacer Coin for use by theater and other commanders as well.

The C130E (Pacer Coin) Aircraft was called to support Peacekeeping operations in Bosnia. The Pacer Coin missions were so vital to the war effort. Helping to identify and record the history of the tragic events that took place in Bosnia. The men of the Air force under Pacer Coin missions worked tireless to keep our country safe. The missions were numerous and flight times were long, The Pacer Coin project was retired in 1998

I was a happy camper, knowing that the right person, Mr. Bentley with his knowledge of the Pacer Coin Project would see me this morning in his office. I passed three CI30 aircraft, warming up for flight. I was excited, and I felt that I was part of something bigger that I can describe. Pilots were adjusting the aircraft propellers for maximum takeoff. I was well behind the flight line but I could hear the roar of those mighty props.

Mr. Bentley greeted me as those we had been friends for years. He was around 45 years old and smoked a pipe. After introduction we sit down in his office behind the flight line. He had a modest office along side the offices of the USAF. He offered me a cup of coffee, not any cup, but a cup of the best coffee a man could ask for. I mentioned about the pilots adjusting their propellers on the C130'S aircraft and Mr. William Bentley was happy to explain the success of the Lockheed C130 Hercules. He said that the propeller is varied by blade angle, which is controlled by the throttles from 0-34 degrees, but in Alpha range, the propeller's governor is attempting to maintain a constant speed of 1020 RPM. Conversely, the alpha range is from 34-90 degrees. Pitch and blade angle are often used interchangeably.

I was truly impressed about his knowledge of the Lockheed C130 Hercules. The two of us then addressed the progress of the Pacer Coin project. He was willing to work with our group to help us while we were at this Lockheed facility. The project was just getting off the ground and needed a group of young engineers to help in Safety and Project Management. Here, I had found the key with Mr. Bentley's help. Not only was he already working with people of importance in the **USAF**, but He knew the Pacer Coin Project well. Mr. Rey Rivas knew the strength of my leadership and approved of me assembling a team of excellent people for the Pacer Coin Project. I left Mr. Bentley office with a blessing; yes I was reminded about my Space and Faith Journey that I was on.

I was proud of my team of excellent engineers; I had preciously learned always to show respect for each person, to draw on their expertise, and always lead the team with a soft, put a firm understanding of what the outcome we were to achieve. To be a good leader, one must delegate responsibility to trustworthy subordinates, and confront those who are doing wrong, and lead by accepting the responsibility for my actions. May I hold myself to a higher standard of accountability, and may I lead by serving my **Lord.**

Mr. Bentley would be working with Lockheed and the Air force. All other engineers and management personal would help in The Pacer Coin Project. We worked as a team under Top Secret conditions with the Department of Defense (DOD). The Pacer Coin Project has now expanded its use, and I will cover the future and use of this project, which is now public knowledge.

On the weekends we would take short trips to refresh ourselves and learn about California. We visited a lot of wine markets, and huge fishing docks filled with fishing boats. There one could rent a small sail boat to sail the bay waters. Being a good hand at sailing we had a lot of fun sailing and getting a sun tan to boot. To finish off a great day, one must have the best sea food one could ask for at a great sea-food dinner. I will never forget these adventures with my friends.

When Slovenia and Croatia declared their independence from Serbian-dominated Yugoslavia, the Serbians fought to maintain control. To keep the fighting from spreading, the United Nations imposed an arms embargo and mediated a cease-fire. The Air Force unit of the Pacer Coin was called to support peacekeeping operations in Bosnia as part of Operation Joint Guard from August 1997 through December 1997. The unit deployed one aircraft and 130 personnel to provide reconnaissance support to the region with its Pacer Coin capability. The airman of this unit did not return home until after 104 days of service. (By GlobalSecurity.Org).

The Air Force Unit of the Pacer Coin was used for reconnaissance support in Peru. Relations were tense between the US and Peru, when the United States took the lead in condemning Mr. Fujimori 's seizure of Peru and stopped aid to Peru. After the US Pacer Coin Unit was sent to do reconnaissance missions for The Drug Enforcement Administration. The C-130 Aircraft came under attack by the Peruvian Air force. Firing warning shots at the C130 while the plane was heading for home base. The passenger door was damaged so bad, causing one Airman to be forced out of the Airplane and never recovered. The Peruvian officials, Apologized for everything. President Bush cancelled all relations with Peru and brought back the C-130 aircraft to the USA. (Article by the New York Times.)

Maintaining constant surveillance is vital to the United Stated. This has lead to Eletro-optical sensor payloads combine with sophisticated digital signal processing to create persistent- surveillance capabilities able to look backwards and forwards through time. This is possible now and is being applied in the United Stated. The Pacer Coin Surveillance and Reconnaissance Program have lead our Nation to new programs, new and wonderful. Take the SkEye WAPS from Eibit Systems in Halfa, Israel, provides situational awareness of on-the-ground intelligence data, and enables a large number of users to receive real- time, high resolution imagery and can go back in time. (Article from Military & Aerospace.)

After two more months or so we finished what we had agreed to do for the Air Force and Lockheed Air Craft Service Corp. We were not amazed at the future of the Pacer Coin ability to do its duty. The US Air Force with numerous serviceman and flights of the Pacer Coin Project serviced our Nation well.

I was blessed to be a part of History on my Space and Faith Journey, what an adventure we all had, and what new adventure lies ahead for us all?

The Bell Family (L to R) My Mother, Father, Uncle Floyd,
Aunt Glayds, and my Grandfather Bell with wife Mary.

My Country Home

At the Old Oak Tree where I was born.

My Family (L to R) Me, my Wife Susan ,Jeff, Chris, and Craig.

My Two Sisters and Me (L to R) Betty, Me and Joann.

My Son Bryan. Picture taken after Space Shuttle Columbia STS-107 Disaster.

My First Mentor Miss Sheldon

The Ingleside Mustangs

"I am in the Army now"

Praise Worship at Laity Lodge. (from L-R) Front roll,
5th person standing, me wearing a dark shirt)

A Family Gathering. (L-R) Me , my Father and Mother.

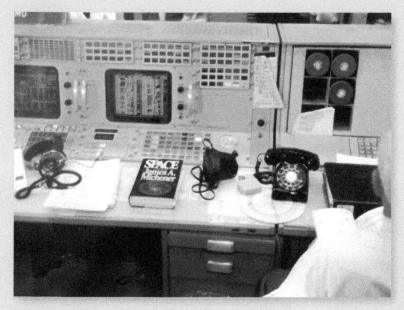

Space by James Mitchner.

The National Aeronautics and Space Administration
Lyndon B. Johnson Space Center

Presents the

GROUP ACHIEVEMENT AWARD

to

BILLY L. BELL

SAIL GNC Test Station Project Team
Lockheed Electronics Company, Inc.

In recognition of their outstanding achievements in the design and development of the Guidance, Navigation, and Control Test Station for the Shuttle Avionics Integration Laboratory.

Signed and sealed at Houston, Texas
this month of June
Nineteen hundred and seventy-eight

Christopher C. Kraft
Director

NASA GNC SAIL Project Award

The National Aeronautics and Space Administration

Presents the

Group Achievement Award

to   Bill Bell

Voice Command System Flight Demonstration Development Team

In recognition of their exceptional professional efforts, resourcefulness, and outstanding accomplishments in the planning, development, and performance of the Voice Command System Flight Experiment on STS-41.

Signed and sealed at Washington, D.C.
the ninth of March
Nineteen Hundred and Ninety One.

Administrator, NASA

NASA Award, Voice Command

Lockheed Engineering and Management Services Company, Inc.

Group Achievement Award

Presented to

B. L. BELL

For outstanding achievement in the development and integration of JSC payloads for the Shuttle STS 41G flight, October 5 through 13, 1984. Your contribution was an integral factor in the successful operation of the IMAX Camera, Large Format Camera, Orbital Refueling System, and OSTA 3 payloads, providing a firm technical foundation for future space projects of this type.

M. E. White
Engineering Technology and Analysis
Branch Director

H. S. Bowes
NASA/JSC Engineering and Science
Program Manager

Lockheed Achievement Award

OUTSTANDING SERVICE AWARD

PRESENTED TO

Bill Bell

FOR DEDICATION TO THE PROFESSION OF MANAGEMENT
AND TO THE CONCEPT AND PRACTICE OF FREE ENTERPRISE
"THANK YOU"

THE NATIONAL MANAGEMENT ASSOCIATION

LOCKHEED HOUSTON CHAPTER

J. M. Parks
PRESIDENT

SECRETARY

5/22/86
DATE

NMA Outstanding Award

LYNDON B. JOHNSON SPACE CENTER
HOUSTON, TEXAS

The Saturn Rocket At Johnson Space Center, Houston Texas.

Spacewalkers Working in Space

Space Shuttle 41C with Lift-off

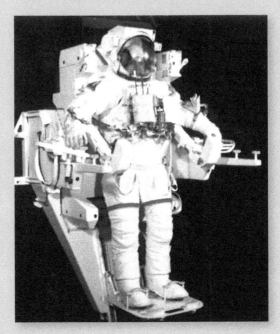

Astronut Mc Candless in the MMU

Lockheed Aircraft Service Company

A Division of Lockheed Corporation
P.O. Box 33 Ontario California 91761

6 March 1985   1312-85-DLH0011

Commander
Det. 4, 2762d LSS (AFLC)
P.O. Box 33
Ontario, California 91761

Attention: K.M. McNellis

Subject: Pacer Coin, COMSEC Access List

The following named personnel require access to COMSEC controlled documents
pertaining to Pacer Coin II aircraft kit, SOW No. AZSW-5014-PC-L39.

NAME	SECURITY CLEARANCE	EMPLOYEE NO.	SSAN
Steve Rice	Secret	372395	479-54-6238

LOCKHEED AIRCRAFT SERVICE COMPANY

[signature]

D.L. Hicks
Program Manager

DLH:djh

CC: MSgt. Brodowski
     G.R. O'Bryan
     T.H. Scarborough
     B.   Bell
     S.   Rice

Lockheed Aircraft Pacer Coin

Lockheed Engineering and Management Services Company, Inc.

Group Achievement Award

Presented to

B. L. BELL

FOR DILIGENCE, INITIATIVE, AND CREATIVITY IN SUPPORTING THE NOVEMBER 1984 RETRIEVAL OF THE WESTAR AND PALAPA SPACECRAFT. IN SPITE OF THE COMPRESSED SCHEDULE, AND BECAUSE OF THE CONSIDERABLE EXTRA EFFORT EXPENDED BY THE GROUP, THIS RETRIEVAL MISSION WAS ACCOMPLISHED WITH THE USUAL HIGH STANDARDS.

THE SUCCESSFUL ACCOMPLISHMENT OF THIS MISSION WAS AN HISTORIC EVENT AND PAVES THE WAY FOR THIS VERY IMPORTANT APPLICATION OF THE SHUTTLE IN THE FUTURE.

B. O. Lippert
Experiments Systems Department
Manager

M. E. White
Engineering Technology and Analysis
Branch Director

D. G. Probe
Applied Mechanics Department
Manager

H. N. Bowes
NASA/JSC Engineering and Science
Program Manager

Achievement Award-For Retrieval of the Westar and Palapa Spacecraft

National Aeronautics and
Space Administration

Lyndon B Johnson Space Center
Houston, Texas
77058

NASA

EA-88-98   DEC 2 1988

Mr. Bill L. Bell
Lockheed Engineering and Sciences Company
2400 NASA Rd. 1
Houston, TX 77058

Dear Bill:

As you know, during the investigation of the Challenger accident, the
Rogers Commission recommended that NASA consider the addition of a Crew
Escape System that would allow the crew to escape during "controlled
gliding flight."

During the past 2 years, you have worked very diligently on the Crew
Escape System for the Orbiter vehicle. As a result of your dedication and
hard work, the Escape System was ready for the STS-26 flight and all
subsequent flights. You should feel a great sense of accomplishment as
part of the team that was able to design, develop, test, and install a new
system in such a short period of time.

Your dedicated support and hard work is a credit to the entire Government-
contractor crew escape team. As team leaders, we wish to thank you for
your excellent contributions in support of this monumental effort.

William A. Chandler
Assistant for NSTS
Engineering Directorate

Col. Steven R. Nagel
Astronaut Office

Robert R. Rice
Crew Escape Project Engineer
Orbiter Project Engineering Office

Shuttle Crew Escape Team Member

"The Lone Piper" Picture taken at Gretna Green, Scotland, Here the "Bell"
Clan came from the Highlands and Settled here. This is my Story.

114

Chapter 12

SHUTTLE STS-6

This was the maiden flight of the Space Shuttle Challenger. Launched from Kennedy Space Center on April 4, 1983. This mission deployed the first tracking and data relay Satellite TDRS-1 into orbit. It Landed at Edwards Air Force Base on April 9, 1983.

STS-6 was the first mission to have a space walk and the first mission for the Extravehicular Mobility Unit (EMU), a special suit designed for the astronauts for their spacewalks.

The flight crew: Commander-Paul J. Weitz, Pilot- Karol J. Bobko. Mission Specialist 1 Story Musgrave, and Mission Specialist 2 Donald H. Peterson.

The EMU was a special space suit needed for astronauts for their protection when they were out side of the space shuttle. They were dressed so to speak, for spacewalking. The suits were white in color, custom made for each astronaut. The EMU was built with 14 layers of fabric to protect each astronaut on their Extravehicular Activity (EVA). Protection was for pressure, thermal, microgravity, and micrometeoroid damage to name a few.

The EMU was built at Johnson Space Center, and has 18 separate parts. It has the ability to sustain an astronaut on their space walks. The EMU when fully assembled becomes a nearly complete short-term spacecraft for one person. It even provides cooling, drinking water, food, electrical power and communications to name a few.

The spacewalkers for this mission were Story Musgrave, and Donald Peterson. Looking back in chapter 7, I introduced Story Musgrave. At that time I was dating his ex-wife Patricia, and I met Story Musgrave one afternoon. He was picking up his special motorcycle that he kept in the garage at Patricia's home. We talked about small things and I wished him well in his space adventures. Now he will be on this Shuttle Mission as one of the spacewalkers, a historical first for all mankind. When I look back in time, my journey in space and faith has brought me to appreciate knowing all the people that are now in the records book. The two space walkers were busy getting suited up for their EVA in the space shuttle, while the first Tracking and Data Relay Satellite (TDRS-1) was positioned in the cargo bay. It was a long and a heavy payload and when it was moved up right and in position, a single rocket attached to the satellite would launch it into its proper orbit. But the satellite failed to go into its proper orbit. A team of engineers at Goddard Space Center worked for nearly 3 months using 6 one- pound thrusters on the errant satellite to push the satellite 8,600 miles higher in space into its proper orbit. The TDRS-1 far exceeded its intended lifespan when it was retired in 2010.

After the launch of the satellite was over the astronauts were ready for their space walks. The EVA lasted for 4 hours, 18 minutes.

The two astronauts were eager to do their spacewalks as they exited the door of the shuttle and into space. They were to do an evaluation of their MMU space suits for flexibility and durability. Also they were to use tools to tighten or loosen Shuttle hardware. They were tethered to keep them safe as they walked/floated along the outside of the shuttle cargo bay. They looked down from the shuttle and could see the Mexican Coast line below. The mobility of their MMU was great.

The astronauts had ample time in the Neutral Buoyancy Lab, a large deep pool of water, for their spacewalking training at **NASA** JSC. I was there to record and make sure all went as planed for safety procedures on their up-coming spacewalks. Astronaut Story Musgrave would take the lead on his Spacewalk.

Their time outside of the space shuttle may have been limited, but the experience would remain with these men for the rest of their lives. "You remember little things like sound," Musgrave told a post-flight pres conference. "Even though there's a vacuum in space. If you tap you fingers together, you can hear that sound because you've set up a harmonic within the space suit and the sound reverates within it. I can still hear that sound today". But the main impression is visual: seeing the totality of humanity within a single orbit; it's a history lesson and a geography lesson; a sight like you have never seen.

The space walkers first task was to tether them selves to guide wires running alongside each side of the payload bay walls. The two space walkers now began their evaluations of their space suits for comfort, dexterity, ease of movement, and the performance of the suit it self. Astronaut Peterson was not happy with the suit's gloves. The gloves are hard to work with he said. Despite this, both astronauts reported that the suits mobility enabled them to satisfactorily accomplish each of their tasks.

For without Musgrave and Peterson's EVA, the complex future steps in space walking, such as the Repair of Solar Max, the serving of the Hubble Space Telescope, and the assembly of the International Space Station, would be far more difficult. With out the TDRS Communication Satellite, the crews of the Space Shuttle and the International Space Station would be severely limited in their ability to transmit voice and data back to earth.

Story Musgrave will fly on future missions on the Space Shuttle in 1985, 1989, 1991, 1993 and 1996 and I was a part of this grand adventure.

SHUTTLE STS-7 AND STS-41-G

Shuttle Mission STS –7 was launched on June 18, 1983 with a liftoff at 7:33 am from The Kennedy Space Center. It was the first mission that included a woman astronaut named Sally K. Ride and up to this time, the largest crew of 5 people. President Ronald Regan also sent his personal favorite Jelly Belly Beans with the astronauts.

We will follow Astronaut Sally K. Ride on her two Shuttle Missions STS-7 and STS-41-G. She was prepared to go as a Specialist on her third Mission on STS-61-M, when the Space Shuttle Challenger disaster occurred.

The crew of STS-7 included Robert L. Crippen as Commander, Fredrick Hauck as Pilot. Sally Ride, John Fabin, and Norman Thagard as Mission Specialist.

Two communications satellites – Anik C2 for Telesat of Canada, and Palpa B1 of Indonesia were deployed successfully during the first two days of the mission. This mission deployed the Satellites using the payload Assist Module (PAM). The PAM using a spin motor for spinning the satellite to create inertia and then with a rocket attached putting it into its proper orbit.

This mission also carried the first Shuttle Pallet Satellite (SPAS-1) built by the West German Aerospace Firm Messerschmit. The SPAS-1 was designed to operate in the payload bay or be deployed by the Remote Manipulator System (RMS) as a free flying satellite. It carried ten experiments to study formation of metal alloys in micro gravity, the Operation of heat pipes, instruments for remote sensing observations, and a mass spectrometer to identify various gages in the payload bay. It was deployed by the (RMS) and flew above the Challenger for several hours. It performed various maneuvers, while a camera mounted on SPAS-1 took pictures of the orbiter.

Sally K. Ride was responsible for operating the RMS to deploy and retrieve the Shuttle Pallet Satellite. SPAS-1 on this mission. While in orbit a window was damaged non- critically by space debris. This is a common situation where more Shuttles were damaged non-critically in different places, by space debris. The space walkers were always in danger of space debris.

The Shuttle landed on June 24, 1983, at Edwards Air Force Base. The mission lasted 6 days, 2 hours, and 23 minutes.

I was working at the Shuttle Avionics Integration Laboratory (SAIL) when Astronaut Sally Ride came in to use the Laboratory. This was my first meeting with her; she was using the lab before the Shuttle STS-7 flight. I welcomed her to our facility; Sally Ride said she was here to practice for her up-coming flight on Challenger. I have a **NASA** picture of her that she signed for me. I still have the picture of her and will present in my book.

We also meet later on at the Canadram-1 or Remote Manipulator System (RMS) Facility at Johnson Space Center. Sally was there to practice for her up-coming Shuttle Mission on STS-7. We became good friends working together for her two Shuttle Missions at Johnson Space Center. I was blessed to have known Sally K. Ride. She was eager to learn as my team prepared her for her mission.

For Shuttle Mission STS –41-G, this was the second and last mission for Sally K. Ride that was launched on October 5th 1984. On board were seven crewmembers, the largest flight crew ever to fly to fly on a single spacecraft at that time. They included Commander Robert L. Crippen, Pilot John A. McBride, and three-mission specialist – David C. Leestma, Sally K. Ride and Kathryn D. Sullivan and two-payload specialist, Paul Scully-Power and Marc Garneau, the first Canadian in space. The mission also marked the first time two female astronauts had flown together. Sally K. Ride and Kathryn D. Sullivan were child-hood friends.

Nine hours after liftoff, the Earth Radiation Budget Satellite (ERBS) was deployed from the payload bay, by the Remote Manipulator System. (RMS). With it's on board thrusters boosted it into orbit 350 miles above the earth. ERBS was the first of three planned satellites designed to measure the amount of energy received from the Sun and reradiated into space. It also studied the seasonal movement of energy from the tropics to the Polar Regions.

Astronaut Sally K. Ride would demonstrate her skills using the RMS.

My Safety Team was responsible for her training on the RMS for the mission. Later on this fine astronaut would serve on the Rogers Commission that was set up to find the cause for the Shuttle STS-51L Disaster. Sally Ride was assigned to investigating both of the Shuttle's accidents on the Shuttle Challenger and later on the Shuttle Columbia disaster.

Astronaut Kathryn Sullivan became the first American woman to walk in space, a certified Space Walker. She and fellow astronaut Leestma performed a three-hour space walk (EVA) on October 11, demonstrating the Orbital Refueling System (ORS) and proving the feasibility of refueling satellites in orbit.

Astronaut and Payload Specialist Scully Power, an employee of the U.S. Naval Research Lab, performed a series of oceanography observations during this mission. Astronaut Garneau conducted a series of experiments by the Canadian government, called CANEX, related to medical, atmospheric, climate, materials, and robotic science.

The Shuttle landed at the Shuttle Landing Facility at Kennedy Space Center on October 13, 1984.

Astronaut Sally K. Ride left **NASA** in 1987 to work at Stanford University. She has an Elementary School that is named after her in my hometown of The Woodlands, Texas.

SPACE SHUTTLE STS41B, STS41C, AND STS-51A WITH WELLNESS CENTER

The Shuttle Challenger STS-41B was launched on February 3, 1984 at the Kennedy Space Center. It was estimated that 100,000 people attended the launch. The crew for this launch included Commander Vance D. Brand, pilot Robert L. Gibson, and Mission specialist Bruce McCandless II, Ronald E. McNair and Robert L. Stewart.

Two communications satellites were deployed about 8 hours after launch. The Westar 6 was for American Western Union, and Papala B2, for Indonesia. However, the Payload Assist Modules (PAM) for both satellites malfunctioned, placing them into a lower-than -planned orbit. Both satellites Were retrieved successfully in November 1984 during STS-51A.

On the fourth day of the mission, astronauts McCandless and Stewart performed the very first untethered spacewalk while they were suited up in their Manned Maneuvering Unit (MMU). McCandless ventured out 320 feet from the orbiter, while Stewart tested the "work station" or foot restraint at the end of the Remote Manipulator System (RMS). On the seventh day of the mission, both astronauts performed another spacewalk (EVA) to practice capture procedures for the Solar Maximum Satellite (SMS) retrieval operation, which was planned for the next Shuttle Mission of STS-41-C.

I worked with Mc Candless for his Spacewalk for safety and mission assurance. He is an Astronaut that was receptive to new ways of doing things. I enjoyed working with this fine man. I knew that he would always appreciate my help. I have several pictures of Mc Candless while he was doing his spacewalk, he was "free as a bird" This is the way that this man felt in Space. "I was more favored than the birds." He replied.

The MMU was designed and built by Lockheed Martin Corp. My team and I were a part of history. We had the job of keeping track of all safety issues for the MMU. This was a tool for the Astronauts use in their Spacewalks, to allow them to work in Space completely free and unthered. Looking back, I am so proud of my safety team, working under tight schedules, and never complaining about their role to make the MMU safe for any astronaut to use.

Lockheed Martin Marietta Corp was awarded the Collier Trophy in 1984 for the development of the MMU. I am proud of all the teams that made it possible for this Trophy, the MMU has made a place in history.

The MMU is an astronaut propulsion unit; it allowed the astronauts to perform untechered space walks or EVA at a distance from the Shuttle. The MMU was used in practice to retrieve a pair of faulty communications satellites, the Westar V1 and Palapa B2, for an up-coming Shuttle Mission STS-51A.

The German built- Shuttle Pallet Satellite (SPAS), originally flown on STS-7, became the first satellite that was to be refurbished and carried back into space. But remained in the cargo bay due to a problem with the Remote Manipulator System (RMS).

The Shuttle landed on February 11, 1984, at Kennedy Space Center (KSC).

The Shuttle Challenger STS-41-C

The Space Shuttle Challenger STS-41-C was launched at Kennedy Space Center on April 6, 1984. The five-member crew included, Commander Robert L. Crippen, Pilot Francis R. Scobee, Mission Specialists George D. Nelson, James D. Van Hoften and Terry J. Hart.

The Space Shuttle Challenger STS-41C was the very first shuttle to make a direct ascent trajectory of 299 statute miles high in the sky. This included using the Shuttle Rockets and a lot of pre- planning by experts.

The main objective of this mission was to capture and repair the Solar Maximum Mission Satellite (SMM).

The Manned Maneuvering Unit (MMU) will allow an astronaut to fly untechered as a Spacewalker. The unit latches to the Spacesuit Extravehicular Mobility Unit Backpack and can be donned and doffed by an astronaut unassisted. The MMU will have a 35 mm still photo camera operated by the astronaut during operations. The two MMUs are located in the forward section of the orbiter payload bay.

Now it is time to capture and repair the Solar Maximum Satellite (SMS). This satellite in orbit was placed there, February 14, 1980 by a Delta Rocket. The SMS had "blew" three fuses in its attitude control system, forcing engineers at **NASA** Goddard Space Flight Center to wait for a mission like STS-41-C for repairs.

To conduct the repair mission, The Shuttle will have made a direct accent to 299 statute miles. Then following the deployment of the Long-Duration Exposure Facility on flight day two, Commander Robert L. Crippen and Pilot Dick Scobee will maneuver the Shuttle higher by another 4-10 miles, or to the altitude of the SMS. Then astronaut Hart can reach out with the remote arm and grapple the SMS satellite to be maneuvered into the cargo bay for repairs by astronauts Nelson and Hoften. The repairs should give Solar Max two additional years of effective operations.

On day 5, Astronauts Nelson and Van Hoften will make another EVA to replace the faulty electronics unit. A replacement electronics unit is installed and finally success for the Solar Max Satellite.

Astronaut Hart will use the remote arm to pick up the Solar Max Satellite and hold it off to the side of the Shuttle. The next day Astronaut Hart will position the SMS satellite with the use of the Remote Arm above the Space Shuttle. Then after receiving word from the Goddard Space Flight Center that all is well with the Solar Max. Hart will direct the Remote Arm to release the Solar Max Satellite. The SMS is now in its proper orbit. The astronauts will keep the shuttle about 300 ft away from the SMS for approximately eight hours. The time will be used for testing the SMS for operational readiness.

This was a valuable effort of capturing and repairing the Soar Max Satellite. This was history making, a time of celebration. The cost of this brave mission has been estimated at about $48 million. The cost of a replacement satellite, including the launch cost of the Shuttle would be approximately $235 million. I would say with certainty, this mission paid for it self many times over. Shuttle STS-41-C landed on April 13, 1984, at Edwards Air force Base, California.

Space Shuttle STS 51-A was launched from Florida's Kennedy Space Center (KSC) at 7: 15 am EST, November 8, 1984. This was less than a month after STS-41-B flight. This was the 14th flight for NASA Space Shuttle Program and the second flight of Space Shuttle Discovery.

STS-51-A marked the first time a shuttle deployed two communications satellites, and retrieved from orbit two other communications satellites.

The five-person crew for this Space Shuttle Mission included Frederick H. Hauck, commander with pilot David M. Walker, with Anna Lee Fisher as Flight Engineer and two-mission specialist; Joseph P. Allen, and Dale A. Gardner.

In Frederick Hauck's mind, the Space Agency had shoot itself in the foot by creating the illusion that Mission 51A would be a piece of cake, a walk in the park. "There is no sense in trying to tell the taxpayers that what you are doing is easy." "He said because it isn't easy." "Any implication that it's easy is a disservice to everyone". Frederick Hauck was livid and said "if we get one of there satellites back," He told the NASA Press Affairs Office, "it'll be amazing, and if we get both of them back, it'll be a Miracle." Here Frederick Hauck was expressing his religion. I knew Frederick Hauck well enough to learn that he was a Man of Faith.

I worked close with all of the astronauts; named on this mission, but my favorite one's were Anna Lee Fisher, Joseph P. Allan, and Frederick Hauk. They both gave so much of them selves in preparing for this mission. They worked as if they had already accomplished their mission. I was dedicated to helping each astronaut in Safety and Mission Assurance (SMA). I was given a signed **NASA** picture from the entire crew of STS-51A.

On the second day of this mission, a communications satellite ANIK-D2 was successfully launched from the cargo bay using the Payload Assist Modules (PAM). On The third day of the mission another satellite, Syncom IV-1 also known as Leasat was successfully launched using the (PAM).

With the deployment of the two communication satellites now successful in orbit, the crew will now focus on the two satellites to be recovered, Palapa B2 and Westar 6. The two satellites were in their wrong orbit and were not communicating, as they should. The two satellites were huge; each one was 22 feet in height by 7 ft. round.

The Space Shuttle began a series of maneuvers to meet up with first of the two satellites to be recovered. On day five of the mission, the Shuttle rendezvoused with Palapa B2. Astronauts, Joseph Allen and Dale Gardner performed a walk in space, (EVA) to capture the Palapa B2.

A very important device was designed and built by Lockheed Martin to help capture satellites. It was called the Stinger (Apogee Kick Motor Capture Device). This device would be inserted into a satellite's apogee motor nozzle by an astronaut, to slow the rotation of the satellite. Astronaut Joseph Allen would use this device to capture the first satellite. But before inserting the Stinger, a problem occurred when astronaut Dale Gardner could not attach the Remote Arm (RMS) to the satellite. This is when Joseph Allen acted as in training and inserted the Stinger to slow the rotation of the satellite. This allowed Allen to Man Handle this satellite and between the two astronauts, and with astronaut Anna Fisher help on the RMS, the astronauts were able to place the satellite into the cradle in the cargo bay of the Shuttle. This exhausting effort took about two hours of extreme effort, because this satellite was rotating and tumbling in space.

My team and I were responsible for the Safety and Mission Assurance (SMA) on this flight as well as the Engineering Safety work on the Stinger.

The satellite to capture next was the Westar 6 on the following day by Joseph Allen and Dale Gardner. Both were ready to capture the satellite on their walk in space (EVA). Joseph Allen again used the Stinger to slow the rotation of the satellite. With Dale Gardner's help, both worked as a team and were able to capture and place the satellite into the cradle in the cargo bay of the Shuttle. Following Westar 6 recovery, Gardner humorously held up a "for sale sign" as if trying to find someone to purchase the malfunctioning satellites. The Westar satellite was indeed later sold to Hong Kong based-AsiaSat.

In Mission Control at NASA, Johnson Space Center, a celebration was heard beyond their doors. When the last Communication Satellite Westar 6 was safely recovered from the depths of space and placed safely into the cargo bay of the Shuttle. The Commander of this mission, Frederick Hauck was correct when he said this was a Miracle.

The Satellite recoveries on STS-51A were the last untethered spacewalks and marked the last use of the Manned Maneuvering Unit. A new system was developed in 1994 called the Simplified Aid for EVA Rescue (SAFER) and was tested on STS-64. On all subsequent spavewalks conducted by NASA and the Soviet/Russian space agencies, all astronauts were tethered to the craft by some means.

The Shuttle made a safe landing at Kennedy Space Center on November 16, 1984. Footage of the landing was used in a Imax Movie – The Dream is Alive.

The NASA Press Affairs Office was now expressing how difficult and dangerous this mission STS-51A really was. They celebrated the news by saying "The recovery of the two communications satellites was truly "A MIRACLE" and I agreed.

The Lockheed Wellness Center was a dream come true for all of Lockheed Employees. The dream began in 1986 and come to exist in 1988. I was given the honor by Lockheed Engineering and Science to manage and lead a team for a new Wellness Center. I was blessed to have this assignment, The wellness Center was selected for the **NASA** Excellent Award in 1989. I will tell you about our team work and the service we provided for Lockheed. First after selecting my team, I had a vision of what the Wellness Center would become. I picked the YMCA for my inspiration. The YMCA was a proven organization and met the goals of our team principles, which are to build in oneself a healthy spirit, mind and body. A proven leader must have a servant spirit to begin with, this leader must hold himself to a higher standard. Our team proved themselves worthy and finished on time. The Wellness Center was up and running in 1988, and the Wellness Center was on the list for The **NASA** Excellent Award in 1989.

.

Chapter 15

SPACE SHUTTLE CHALLENGER DISASTER: STS-51L

This is the story of the final flight of Space Shuttle Challenger and the loss of the entire Shuttle Crew. I will not tell you about the details of how each astronaut perished, but will honor each person on this mission. What caused this great tragic event to happen is what we will bring forth.

STS-51L was launched from Kennedy Space Center, on January 28, 1986. The crewmembers were Commander Dick Scobee, Pilot Michael J. Smith, Mission Specialist Ellison S. Onizuka, Judith A. Resnik and Ronald E. McNair, and Payload Specialists Christa McAuliffe.

On a beautiful frosty morning, a day packed with people wanting to see the launch. At first everything seemed to be normal, as the Shuttle roared to life and lifted off. Then as the Shuttle was almost 8-10 mile high it began to break apart, as people in the **NASA**-Kennedy Space Center viewing stand watched in horror as the Spacecraft disintegrated over the Atlantic Ocean, off the cost of Cape Canaveral, Florida at 11:39 am. EST.

I was watching the launch of STS-51L at **NASA**, Johnson Space Center at Mission Control Center. Challenger was now moving at nearly 2,000 mph and more than 10 miles high. It was enveloped in a mammoth ball of hell and broke to pieces. As we were watching, Challenger had exploded into a huge red and yellow ball of flame. White- hot chunks of it were falling into the sea leaving streams of smoke in the sky. There was total silence from Mission Control, and then some one said, "On my **God**".

I personally knew each crew- member on this mission; so I felt the explosion and the searing heat that they must have experienced and their friendships will stay with me forever. I do not know yet how to express myself, other than to personally feel grief for each friend. I thought, May our **lord** welcome all the Crewmembers into his Home. A lone parachute was spotted by the people coming down from a C130 Aircraft. We all knew at **NASA** that it was a military paramedic coming to help, if any one did survive the fall. **NASA** would be sending divers down soon to investigate the accident.

Much later the crew compartment and many other vehicle fragments were recovered from the ocean floor. The debris from the Shuttle would wash ashore as the probe continues. The security at the Kennedy Space Center was on high alert, **NASA** had to make sure that no one was taking pictures that were not authorized, or stealing objects from the disaster. There were no escape system provided for the Shuttle. This came later; my team and I played a vital part for the Safety and Mission Assurance (SMA) for a new Space Shuttle Escape System, "The Escape Pole" which I will cover later on in another chapter.

The disaster resulted in a 32-month hiatus in the shuttle program. And the formation of the Rogers Commission, a special commission appointed by President Ronald Reagan to investigate the accident. The Rogers Commission found NASA's organizational culture and decision making-processes had been key contributing factors to the accident. Thousands of **NASA** and Contractor employees were laid off. I was spared to work on a Shuttle Escape System. This was a hard time in the history of the **NASA** Space Administration. I thank my **Lord** for looking after me in this terrible time at **NASA.**

This mission was to be a celebration for education, planned as the Teacher in Space Project, (TISP) a **NASA** program announced by President Ronald Reagan on August 27, 1984. The teachers would not be members of NASA Astronaut Corps. The teachers would fly as Payload Specialist and return to their classrooms after the flight was ended. More than 11,000 applications were sent to **NASA**. Each teacher would include a potential lesson that would be taught from space while on the Space Shuttle. Christa McAuliffe was chosen from all the others to be the first teacher in Space. She was a high school social studies teacher from Concord, New Hampshire. She planned to teach two 15-minute lessons from the Space Shuttle, but her life was cut short, as were others in this tragic event in history.

Leon Hale was a writer for the Houston Chronicle Paper noted for his style of country writing. He was asked to write an article in the Houston Chronicle covering the This Space Shuttle Disaster. "When the Explosion happened on Tuesday, I wasn't ready for it. What I feel right now is personal grief. Probably in print that will sound maudlin, but they have asked me to write about what I feel and that's what it is, sorrow, No story as big as Space travel could go on with success after success and no failure". Years later I met Leon Hale at his book signing at Barnes and Noble Book Store in The Woodlands Texas. He was an unpretentious person, I learned. He signed my book for me and we had a good chat. I will forever remember this man.

All across our Nation, Churches were having services to honor the crew members of STS-51L. I remember reading about how religion had placed a big part in the life of each person on this flight.

NASA- with President Ronald Reagan had a Special Tribute to the loss of STS-51L Crewmembers. I will always remember this day with my dear wife beside me at **NASA** Johnson Space Center. The President said these immortal words "They slipped the surly bonds of earth to touch the Face of **GOD.**" This was a poem "High Flight" by John Gillespie Magee Jr. This

American pilot flew with the Royal Canadian Air Force during WW11. This is a fitting poem for the loss of all the Shuttle crew also.

What was the root cause of the Space Shuttle Disaster of STS-51L.? It began to show its dangerous effects, during the mission of STS-2. Here serious evidence of hot gas "blow-by" was observed and recorded. This was caused by an o-ring erosion in the Solid Rocket Booster (SRB). **NASA** Managers had known since 1977 that the contractor Morton-Thiokol's design of the SRBs contained a potentially catastrophic flaw in the o-rings, but they had failed to address the problem properly. **NASA** managers also disregarded warnings from Safety Engineers from Morton Thiokol, about the dangers of launching at freezing temperatures, of that mornings launch. **NASA** management also failed to adequately report these technical safety issues to their superiors. This Space Shuttle Disaster has been used as a case study for the Engineering Safety and work-place ethics.

Each of the Space Shuttle's two Solid Rocket Boosters (SRBs) the joints were sealed with two rubber O-rings. After the disaster of the Shuttle, the number of O-rings per field joint was increased to three O-rings. The seals of all the SRBs joints were required to contain the hot, high- pressure gases produced by the burning solid propellant inside, thus forcing them out of the nozzle at the end of each rocket.

Roger Boisjoly worked as a Safety Engineer at the solid-rocket booster manufacturer Morton Thiokol at Wasatch, Utah. Mr Boisjoly knew that he had to stop the Shuttle Launch that morning. He and other Safety Personal began warning as early as 1985 about the joints in the boosters could fail in frigid weather, which it was on this launch date. Then on the eve of January 28, 1986 Mr. Boisjoly and four other co-workers in safety, argued late into the night against the launch. The temperature had fallen to 23 degrees. This was a dangerous game to play with other lives in the balance. In cold temperature, 0-rings in the booster joints would not seal, they said, and could allow flames to reach the rocket's metal casing. This is what they predicted would happen and no one in authority at **NASA** would listen to them.

I met Mr. Boisjoly at Kennedy Space Center in 1985. We both worked in Safety Engineering in supporting **NASA,** so we had a lot in common. Mr. Boisjoly and I would talk about the up-coming Shuttle flight STS-61B in 1985. He did not say a lot, but I enjoyed talking with him and his career with Morton Thiokol. Then for reasons unknown, he opened up about his religion and how it has placed a burden on him to always be mindful of safety first.

The tragedy became a personal burden for him and created a lifelong quest to challenge the bureaucratic ethics that had caused the tragedy. Roger Boisloly challenged everyone at **NASA** and in his company to take his warning to scrub this launch. But no one agreed because he failed to prove his case. How can he prove something that has not happened yet? The burden of proof will be every ones downfall.

A Presidential Commission known as the Rogers Commission was created and charged with investigating the Space Shuttle Challenger disaster of the STS-51L. All of the members of the commission after haring the evidence stated, "This is an accident rooted in history". The report strongly criticized the decision making process that was none by **NASA** and Morton Thiokol. This was a flawed launch decision that led to the disaster of the shuttle and all of the Crew. My friend Sally K. Ride served as a member of the Rogers Commission. She also served on the final dismiss of the Space Shuttle STS-35.

In the investigation that followed the tragedy, Mr. Boisloly became known as a whistle-blower when he furnished internal documents that would prove his case from his company to The Rogers Commission. He had to be honest with him self and bear the burden that would follow. He choose to fight on for justice.

Roger Boisloly was treated badly at Morton Thiokol, and then his friends left him without support. After reading about all the humiliation he suffered simple because he wanted to make sure this tragedy will never happened again. Roger and his family all were suffering together.

Following his testimony at the Presidential Commission, Roger was cut off from Space work at Morton Thiokol and shunned by colleagues and friends. I felt for this man that I had met in 1985; he was a gentle giant of a man. My hart still go out to this man, strong in his faith and convections.

Astronaut Sally Ride, while serving on the panel of the Presidential Commission, was supportive of Roger and hugging him as he was leaving the Commission with a grateful heart. (As told by Roger Boisloly).

Roger Boisloly later would be vindicated for his actions, and awarded the Prize for Scientific Freedom and Responsibility. He went on to speak at more than 300 Universities and civic groups about corporate ethics. Roger was sought after as an expert in forensic engineering.

Roger Boisloly has died from a long battle with cancer. We will always remember this brave man, who had the courage to stand up for his religious convictions.

I will always remember the brave men and women aboard the Space Shuttle STS-51. Each life is scared and will forever shine like a star in the Univerise. From long ago when I was a small boy looking up at the moon, I never invisioned that I would now be looking at these six shinning stars in the heavens above.

Chapter 16

SPACE BY JAMES MICHENER

I went to a meeting at Johnson Space Center to find out about being an extra in an up-coming Television series called "SPACE." I was not sure if I would be picked, but I was interested any-way. The TV Series was to be filmed at Johnson Space Center where I worked. Space, the epic 13- hour mini-series based on James Michener best-selling Novel, Space would be in production for broadcast on the CBS-Television Network soon.

"SPACE" tells the story of a cross-section of fictional characters deeply involved in the U.S. Space efforts. It spans the years from the end of WW11 to the exploration of the moon in the early 1970's. It covers the adventures and exploits of the space pioneers, the headlines making events and the behind-the-scenes struggles and compromises.

After reading the novel Space by James Mitchener, I was thrilled to be a part of this adventure. It was important to be picked for this TV production due to my experience at **NASA**. I went to this meeting and met a lot of people that I knew, who were trying to get a part also in this production. After interviewing I was picked to play a General in the Air Force. Why I was picked is because I was tall and thin enough to meet the requirements, plus I smiled a lot, any way I am here to do my best.

I phoned my dear wife at Mitchell Corp. and she was suppressed and happy for me getting the part. I now had to figure out if I could squeeze

in the time for my acting part, because of my work schedule. It worked out for me; I would play the part of a General on the following weekend.

The cast included: James Garner, Susan Anspach, Beau Bridges, Blair Brown, Bruce Dern, Mellinda Dillon, David Dukes, Harry Hamlin, and Michael York.

I was excited to get picked and got paid too, I was happy to be added to the long list of people in this TV Mini Series called SPACE. I came that morning to the dress/make-up department. When they were through with me; I looked every-bit of a General in the Air Force. Before I knew it, I was in the **NASA** Control Room. (Control Room that directs all Space Flights). I was filmed there looking every bit of a General in the Air force. I had to look serious and not smile a lot.

On another weekend I was prepared to be at NASA- Johnson Space Center real early in the morning. This was a day of filming at the Worlds largest Vacuum Chamber (VC) at **NASA.** One cannot picture this (VC) without being totality mystified, when one opens the large medal doors to the vacuum chamber. This is where **NASA** Space Flight Equipment is put into this large chamber for testing. This morning I will play the part of a local News Reporter from Houston TX. I went into the dress/make-up room and returned as a happy reporter to cover the news of the day.

There was a large group of people/actors already gathered at the Large Vacuum Chamber. There were a lot of people here; all ready to play their part in this TV Series called "Space". You had many news reporters and people with cameras, and many more people just standing around. Certain cast members were in their spot at the entrance of the huge Vacuum Chamber (VC), ready to be introduced by a NASA official. When that happened, camera men/women spring into action along with me, to record the events. The filming took a long time, due to retakes. They picked a perfect spot for filming at the large VC. I used my press/news tablet to record the news in short hand. I had taken many notes before the day was throught.

I have been overseeing test results from Space Flight Equipment for many years in this Large Vacuum Chamber. There is a smaller vacuum chamber located on this **NASA** site also. I picked my Education in Safety Management and Engineering because eventically everything must pass a safety test. I have followed the advice of my mentors on my Space and Faith Journey.

When the actors for SPACE were wrapping things up for the day, they signed my Press/News Tablet, I used for taking notes. Most all of the cast did sign my tablet. I have a lot of pictures of everybody. Actor Bruce Dern was very nice to me; this was his first acting position in a long spell. We all gathered at the NASA Cafateria. I have learned to respect each Actor, and will remember this day of filming for the Television Series "SPACE."

RETURN TO FLIGHT: DISCOVERY STS-26R WITH NASA EXCELLENT AWARD

There were two years and eight months of rebuilding after the Shuttle Challenger exploded. Shuttle STS-26R was declared the "Return to Flight." Employees of **NASA** had been working hard to achieve this goal. Looking back at the Shuttle Challenger Disaster, let me tell you about the layoffs that took place, about half or more of the workforce was laid off at every **NASA** Site. It put a strain on the remaining workers, but being employed and having a place to work was worth it, and again I felt the blessing of our **Lord**. It was only one week after the Shuttle Disaster occurred, that **NASA** started to push for the next Shuttle Launch. "The Space Program must continue," giving hope and insperation to every space employee. I remember the crewmembers on that tragic day, who I knew well. And I am sure that they would agree with me, that the space program must press ahead. But an essential part of moving forward is putting the Challenger accident behind us.

This mission with a crew of 5 astronauts was eager to begin the Return to Flight. Crew Members were as follows, Commander: Frederick H. Hauck, Pilot: Richard O. Coveys, Mission Specialist 1: John M. Lounge, Mission Specialist: 2 David C. Hilmers, and Mission Specialist 3: George D. Nelson.

The Space Shuttle Discovery lifted off from Kennedy Space Center on 29 September 1988. The primary payload for this mission, a Tracking, and Data Relay Satellite (TDRS-C) was successful deployed. Eleven scheduled mid-deck scientific and technology experiments were carried out.

Over the years, Commander Rick Hauck and I have not only worked together professional, but have become good friends. We worked as a team for payload Safety. In chapter 14 we covered the launch of Space Shuttle STS-51A, with Commander Hauck. On this successful mission, two satellites were recovered. It was a "Miracle explained Commander Hauck." This will be the third and last mission for Commander Hauck. I will miss my dear friend at **NASA**.

The nation was ready to celebrate the renewal of the U.S. manned space program. Part of moving ahead is giving the crewmembers of the Challenger disaster a proper place in history. This is what, this shuttle flight STS-26R achieved. The crew experienced a thoughtful tribute to the Challenger with an Air Show over Kennedy Space Center, following the return of the Shuttle. The loss of the Challenger crewmembers meant a lot to this nation, but we have pressed on to 'Return to Flight.' The return of the Space Shuttle STS-26R will now have the Shuttle Escape System, a safe bailout feature, and the redesigned solid rocket boosters were also tested and ready for flight.

The Shuttle Escape System (SES) would be added to every Shuttle. Lockheed Martin Corporation was in charge of this new SES. Lockheed held a Space Conference at the Houston Texas George R. Brown Conference Center to show off the new Shuttle Escape System. It drew thousands of Engineers and Space workers.

I was asked to organize and lead a team to design this new Shuttle Escape System. (SES). There were several teams working on the SES. We were successful in our efforts to have the Shuttle Escape System ready. Our team worked a lot of overtime to finish with our part, which is Safety and

Mission Assurance. The SES consisted of a spring-loaded telescoping 10 ft. long aluminum pole in a curved housing mounted on the mid- deck ceiling. A magazine at the end of the pole held 8 sliding hooks and lanyard assemblies. In an emergency, crewmembers could open the side hatch, deploy the pole, and then slide out along the pole to parachute away from the Shuttle. The crew needed the escape pole to get them below the Shuttle wing before bailing out.

The Shuttle Escape System had been tested and proven to be safe by Navy parachutists with over 66 tests. The pole held up under testing and was certified by NASA.

My team and I were glad that we finished our part of the Shuttle Escape System. I generally finished around eight pm, and I headed for home. The long drive to The Woodlands, Texas was about 80 miles. I had learned to tune my radio to a channel that had a Scottish Minister telling about life in Scotland. This was Alistair Begg, giving hope and insperation to weary travelers like me. Minister Begg was born in Glasgow, Scotland and still has his distinctive Scottish accent. My Great Grandfather was from Scotland, and this made me a true Scott also. I came across a poem that my Great Grandfather loved, and the title is "**Lord** I want to walk the Higher Road with you." I finally arrived home to be welcomed by a loving Wife, this was indeed a blessed homecoming.

This was the first mission that used an all veteran crew since Apollo 11. Each crewmember had flown at least one previous mission.

This was the first spacecraft to fly in space equipped with a Voice Command System, (VCS). A computer capable of recognizing and responding to human speech. The VCS would also control the cameras and monitors that were used by the crew to monitor the Canadarm or mechanical arm, which is mounted in the cargo bay. I worked with the Astronauts for safety training on the Canadarm and the Shuttle Escape Pole as the primary bailout feature. I received a commendation from **NASA** and the Astronauts on this mission. I was given a framed picture with a USA Flag that was carried into space. I will treasure this gift forever.

The crewmembers practiced suiting –up in a new partial-pressure flight suite. They practiced the unstowing and attaching of the Shuttle Escape Pole. The 5-man crew will now pay tribute to the crewmembers lost in the Challenger disaster by their own special Prayer, before returning to Edwards Air Force Base on October 3, 1988.

As the Shuttle came to a halt at Edwards Air Force Base, one could hear the cheers. The nation was ready to press forward again, as the crowd paid tribute to the astronauts. The STS-26R crew with their wives then flew to Ellington Field in Houston, Texas. With over 40,000 cheering people were there to greet the crewmembers as they landed. The 5-member crew was overtaken with a sense of excitement of the cheering crowd and large banners that read "**NASA** and Houston Back on Top to Stay".

Commander Rick Hauck and the other crewmembers positive comments were directed toward the employees of **NASA** and its Contractors, who played a vital role in the Nations Return to Space. "Rick Hauck said that he wished he could take all of you with him". I appreciated his remarks as I remember my friend who said to me "This is my last Shuttle Flight."

It was a mixed emotion for the ones who had lost a loved one in that tragic day of the Shuttle Challenger Disaster. They were proud of the Shuttle Crew of STS-26R, for leading our Nation to Return to Flight, but at the same time they felt their grief and sorrow. A widow of a lost Astronaut said that it's time to look ahead, we must move on in life. Yes the list of names were many that were affected by this disaster. But all were In agreement, that the crewmembers of the Shuttle Challenger are now safe in our **Fathers** keeping.

The Shuttle Escape System is now in the National Air and Space Museum. A fitting place for such an important life- saving device for all Astronauts to use when needed.

I am well pleased with our team and the other teams that made this mission a success. I felt blessed and realized the total commitment of each team members. The Shuttle Mission of STS-26R was more than a Return to Flight, it was a starting point for **NASA** and gave hope to all that were affected by the disaster of the Shuttle Challenger.

In 1989 Lockheed Engineering & Sciences was awarded the **NASA Excellence Award** for Quality and Productivity. This was a competition that included over twenty-eight major **NASA** Contractors. This Excellence Award included the Shuttle Escape System, Lockheed Wellness Center, Shuttle flight Payloads, Technical Information Processing System (TIPS), Total Quality Management, The Voice Command System, and the Foundations Mentoring Program for all employees of Lockheed and **NASA.**

It was an honor to have been picked by **NASA** as a Management Team Leader, along with my valued teams. For the leadership of the Foundations Mentoring Program, (Chapter 10), The Lockheed Wellness Center, (chapter 14) and for the Total Quality Management Program (see chapter 9). I would like to express my team commitment for helping us win the **NASA** Excellent Award.

The **NASA Excellence Award** was presented to me and my teams. We were also awarded a Gold **NASA** Pin, to be displayed on one's coat or suit. This Pin, I hold most dear.

THE HUBBLE SPACE TELESCOPE SHUTTLE STS-31 AND STS-61

Mission STS-31 was launched from Kennedy Space Center on April 24, 1990 at 12:33 PM. The main objective for this mission was to launch the Hubble Space Telescope (HST). The Hubble was named after Edwin Hubble, an American Astronomer who worked at the Mount Wilson Observatory. This great man died in 1953, but not before he found evidence that Galaxies move away from each other, at a constant rate.

The HST is a joint project between **NASA** and the European Space Agency. The Space Telescope Science Institute (STSCI) operates The HST for **NASA**. The length of Hubble is 43.5 feet, maximum diameter is 14 feet, and the weight is 24,500 lbs. The HST is at an average altitude of 307 nautical miles; time to complete one orbit is 97 minutes at a speed of 17, 500 mph.

Lockheed Martin Space Systems in Sunnyvale, Calif. was chosen by **NASA** to design and build the HST. Lockheed also provided Spacecraft Systems Integration. Since the launch of Shuttle STS-31, Lockheed Martin personnel in Sunnyvale and at Goddard Space Flight Center, Md. have helped **NASA** manage the day-to-day spacecraft operations of the Telescope and provided extensive preparation and training for the telescope-servicing missions.

The Hubble Space Telescope is what this Astronaut Crew have been training for, and they were up to the task for STS-31. The Shuttle crew of 5 astronauts and their Positions: Commander Loren J. Shiver, Pilot Charles F. Bolden, Mission Specialist 1 Bruce Mc Candless, Mission Specialist 2 Steven A. Hawley, and Mission Specialist 3 Kathryn D. Sullivan. I worked with this Shuttle Crew for safety and Mission Assurance (S & MA). I also received a beautiful photograph of Bruce Mc Candless floating in Space from this mission.

The Shuttle Crew for STS-31 worked very hard for their up-coming mission. The Astronauts trained using **NASA** Neutral Buoyancy Lab. They trained using a Simulator of a full-scale mockup of the Hubble Space Telescope. The training was tiring but necessary for their mission.

When the Shuttle was in the correct orbit, the Hubble Telescope would be deployed. The HST was designed to operate above the Earth's turbulent and obscuring atmosphere to observe celestial objects at ultraviolet, visible and near-infrared wavelengths. The Shuttle soared to 370 miles, a record height for the crew to use the IMAX Cameras to photograph Earth's large-scale geographic features not apparent from lower orbit. Two IMAX cameras also filmed "Destiny in Space" you may have seen this film.

As the Hubble Telescope was being deployed, one of its solar array panels stopped as it unfurled. Mission Specialist Mc Candless and Sullivan began preparing for a contingency spacewalk in the event that the array could not be unfurled. Then the array finally came free and unfurled by ground control personell at **NASA.**

As a secondary payload included in the cargo bay, was an 11-pound human skull this joint **NASA/DOD** experiment was designed to examine the penetration of radiation into the human cranium during spaceflight.

After months had passed the Hubble Space Telescope was sending an array of images that were somewhat blurred, not as good as they had predicted. The teams studied the images and came to the conclusion that the main focusing mirror had been polished to the wrong specifications. This "spherical aberration" was so miniscule- less than 1/50 the width of a strand of human hair, yet it was enough to blur many of its photos. This meant that another Shuttle Mission was needed to correct the optics on the HST.

The HST is the only telescope that was designed to be maintained in space by the Astronauts. Shuttle mission STS-61 would be next in line to repair the Hubble Telescope.

Space Shuttle Endeavour, STS-61 was launched on December 2, 1993 on launch pad 39B, from Kennedy Space Center. It took 3 years after the launch of Shuttle Mission STS-31 to mount a Shuttle repair mission on the HST. I was blessed to have supported STS-31 and STS-61. With the help from the Hubble Telescope, we now will be able to view **"God's Celestial Handy work".**

The mission of STS-61 had a crew of 7 astronauts, with Commander Richard O. Covey, Pilot, Kenneth D. Bowersox, Payload commander, Story Musgrave, and with Mission Specialist Kathryn C. Thornton, Claude Nicollier, Jeffrery A. Hoffman, and Tom Akers.

This was one of the most challenging and complex manned missions ever attempted. On flight day 2, Endeavour performed a series of burns that allowed the shuttle to close in on the HST. The crew now excited made a detailed inspection of the large payload and checked out the Remote Manipulator Arm (RMA) and their spacesuits. They were now ready for a good nights sleep.

At this time, my memory was going back to the year of 1980. When I first meet Astronaut Story Musgrave, his ex-wife and family. This story was still fresh in my mind, I had been dating his ex-wife Patricia Musgrave and getting to know her family. She was a happy person and easy to get along with. Patricia loved the Galveston Beach, she could swim, waiting for a big wave to help propel her to the shore. We only dated for short time, but I can still remember her kindness and her special smile. Story Musgrave, being a Spacewalker and a doctor was a valuable asset to the Space Program. More than once he has helped his fellow Spacewalkers needing some medical aid. I enjoyed getting to know the children of the Musgrave family, we enjoyed each other's company. I was blessed to have known this family and will always remember their kindness.

On flight day 3 a solar array panel was spotted by Jeffrey Hoffman to be bent at a 90-degree angle. The two solar panels were to be replaced. Now Commander Dick Covey maneuvered Endeavour within 30 feet of the free flying HST. Now Claude Nicollier using the (RMA) to grapple the HST and placed it into the cargo bay of the shuttle.

Space walk no. 1 on flight day 4, Story Musgrave and Jeffrey Hoffman stepped into the cargo bay at 10: 46 pm EST. Hoffman installed a foot restraint platform into the end of the (RMA). This allowed Hoffman to safely work in Space. Story Musgrave installed protective covers on Hubble's aft low gain antenna and on exposed voltage bearing connector covers. The astronauts then opened the HST equipment doors and installed another foot restraint inside the Telescope. Musgrave helped Hoffman into the foot restraint. Hoffman would replace two sets of Rate Sensing Units (RSU). These units contain gyroscopes that help keep Hubble pointed in the right direction. The astronauts then replaced a pair of electrical control units. Now Hubble with eight new fuse plugs to protect the electrical circuits will perform as directed by the ground control employees.

The astronauts had trouble with the latches on the gyro doors, when two of the gyro door bolts would not reset. The ground control unit said it was due a temperature change was the problem. With Musgrave at the bottom of the doors worked on the bolts using a payload retention device.

Hoffman attached to the (RMA) worked at the top of the doors. The two worked together to successful close the doors with top and bottom latches.

Musgrave and Hoffman then prepared for the solar array carrier, which is located at the forward portion of the cargo bay. They attached a foot restraint on the Hubble. This was to assist in the solar array replacement for Tom Akers and Kathy Thornton's up-coming space walk.

Musgrave and Hoffman's spacewalk became the second longest in **NASA'S** history. Lasting 7 hr. and 50 min. A number of space-walks have since surpassed these but, only a few minutes longer.

Space walk number 2 on flight day 5 began on December 5 at 10:35 EST. Astronaut Tomas Akers began installing a foot restraint on the (RMA) for Kathryn Thornton. The astronauts were to replace the two solar arrays on the Hubble.

Spacewalk number 3 on flight day 6 began with astronauts Hoffman and Musgrave. Their mission was to replace the Wide Field Planetary Camera (WFPC). The Camera weight was 620 pounds for the new camera (WFPC2). Ground Controllers then ran a test for 35 minutes, and it was given a higher rating than the previous model, especially in the ultraviolet range, and included its own spherical aberration correction system. Following the (WFPC2) installation, Hoffman changed out two magnetometers on board the HST. This would enable the HST to find its orientation with respect to the Earths magnetic field.

Spacewalk number 4 on flight day 7 began with astronauts Thornton and Akers. The primary task was to replace the high speed Photometer (HSP) on Hubble with the Corrective Optics Space Telescope Axial replacement. (COSTAR). This system would correct Hubble's spherical aberration of the main mirror. This space walk was successful and lasted 6 hours and 50 minutes.

Spacewalk number 5 on flight day 8 began with Musgrave and Hoffman. Right away Musgrave was having trouble with his space suit. His suit failed its initial leak check, and Musgrave performed steps on the 5 psi contingency checklist. He rotated his spacesuits lower arm joints and the suit passed two subsequent leak tests. Musgrave and Hoffman's first task was to replace the Solar Array Drive Electronics (SADE). The astronauts then installed covers on the magnetometers to contain any debris caused by the older magnetometers that were showing signs of UV decay.

During this flight day inside the Shuttle, Hoffman being Jewish displayed and spun a Dreidel (a four sided spinning top) used for the Holiday of Hanukkah. He also brought a travel Menorah with him to celebrate his Jewish holiday on a live televised audience to his homeland in Israel.

Now ground controllers including me were jumping for joy as they heard from **NASA** that it was a go for all systems. The Astronaut crew had accomplished all of the work for the HST, now it was time to return home to their family and friends.

Release of Hubble and the Shuttle landing. Flight day 9 began on December 9, 1993. Hubble was grappled by the Remote Control Arm by Claude Nicollier and deployed the Hubble Space Telescope. Then Commander Dick Covey and pilot Kenneth Bowersox then moved the Shuttle slowly away from Hubble. Everyone was so glad that Hubble was now in space to take beautiful pictures of our solar system and it accomplished more than we ever expected. The images began to show us the inspiring solar system as **"God"** had intended.

This iconic image of the "Pillars of Creation" was taken in 1995 by the HST. It is the most famous astronomical image of the 20th century. It shows a part of the Eagle Nebula where new stars are forming. The tallest pillar is around 4 light-years high. I hope to give you a picture in my book.

The light that the HST views from remote objects only reveals how that object appears when the light left it, not how it appears today. Thus when we look at the Andromeda galaxy 2.5 million light-years from Earth, we see it as it was 2.5 million years old. And with the HST, distant objects are revealed that otherwise can't be seen at all.

When astronomers pointed the HST to a seemingly empty patch of sky in Ursa Major in 1995, for instance, they captured an image of over 3,000 galaxies too distant to be detected by any other telescopes.

I will list the HST servicing missions: #1Shuttle Mission STS-61 in 1993, # 2 Shuttle Mission STS-82 in 1997 # 3 Shuttle Mission STS-103 in 1999, # 4 Shuttle Mission STS-109 in 2002.

The landing of the Shuttle was at the Kennedy Space Center on December 13, 1993.

BUILDING THE SPACE STATION SHUTTLE —STS-37 AND STS-88

Space Shuttle Atlantis STS -37 was launched on April 5, 1991, from Kennedy Space Center. Atlantis will place the Gamma Ray Observatory (GRO) in a 243 nautical mile orbit. It was the largest **NASA** Satellite ever deployed by the space shuttle and its weight was 35,000 pounds. Commanding the flight will be Steve Nagel, Pilot will be Ken Cameron, Mission Specialist Linda Godwin operating the (RMS) mechanical arm, with Jerry Ross and Jay Apt as the two Space Walkers. Apt and Ross will test the prototype equipment designed for STS -37. My team and I worked with Jerry Ross and Jay Apt for Safety and Mission Assurance to reach the goals for their space walks. All of the astronauts were easy to work with, each signed a **NASA** photograph for me. It was a blessing to know and appreciate each Astronaut on my Faith and Space Journey.

The Payload of the Gamma Ray Observatory (GRO) was deployed on the third day in Space. The antenna failed to deploy, but was finally freed and manually deployed by Ross and Apt. This took a lot of manpower, let me tell you, by Ross and Apt, before the satellite was released into space. Steve Nagel took pictures of Ross in space and the pictures were used to welcome travelers to the Space Coast in Orlando Florida. The next day, Apt and Ross moved themselves and equipment about on a Crew and

Equipment Translation Aid (CERTA). This equipment Cart was used in the shuttle cargo bay while working on their space simulation for Space Station Freedom in the near future.

Jerry Ross and three other Astronauts were picked to join the Association of Space Explorers (ASE) to fly to Russia to support Science and Space. They arrived in Moscow in 1990 and later flew to Baikonur in Kazakhstan. They were able to tour the launch site Facility for the heavy-lift Proton Rocket. The very next day two Cosmonauts were to blast off and dock with the Mir Space Station.

I began to thank back on my time working at the Saturn V Rocket facility in New Orleans La. (Covered in Chapter 2) and the Scientists that I had become friends with, like Mr. Rubin. A kindly, but a very secretive man and Wernher Von Braun from the Marshall Space Flight Center in Huntsville, Alabama. This great German Scientist and Rocket Designer with a history of early rocket design during World War 2. He was now in charge of the Saturn V Rocket Program. The Saturn V Rockets would provide the propulsion needed to place a man on the moon. This great scientist was visiting our facility and we met by chance. This quick meeting lead to another meeting later on to form a friendship with this great Scientist. Years later, I was at the Marshall Space Center in Huntsville Alabama on Space Business and I spotted Wernher Von Braun coming towards me, Both of us could not believe that we were meeting again. He smiled at me with a big smile, and said "hello". We had time to meet over coffee and this was the beginning of our renewed relationship. I valued his friendship and he valued mine.

Mr. Rubin a Russian Scientist who came to the U.S. as a young man many years ago was responsible for work on the Saturn V Rocket Program. Mr. Rubin, my dear friend was the one who gave me the recipe for Borach, a Russian Stew. I think often of the people that had an impact on my Space and Faith Journey. We all must treasure our friends we meet along life's way.

The Space News Roundup, NASA's own News Paper, wrote about Texas Gov. Ann Richards and Senator Barbara Mikuiski who came to the Johnson Space Center at a special reception, prior to the launch of Shuttle STS-37. They were there to tell the World that the Space Station would be funded. This meant a lot to this area, and for the space employees, that the Space Station would now be built. Much later I asked for Texas Gov. Ann Richards for special visitor passes to visit the White House and she was more than happy to send them to me.

The Space Shuttle Endeavor STS-88 was launched on December 16, 1998 and was the first Shuttle to start building the International Space Station (ISS). This Space Shuttle carried the American Unity Node in its payload bay, to be mated with a Russia (FGB) Zarya Module built by Boeing and the Russian Space Agency. It was launched on a Russian Proton rocket from the Baikonur Cosmodrome in Kazakhstan Russia in November 1998.

The primary mission objective was to rendezvous with the already launched Zarya Control Module and successfully attach the American Unity Node. This will provide the foundation for the future Space Station components and the start of the International Space Station. Zarya after mating up with the Unity Node will provide propulsion, power and communications. The Unity Node will serve as the main connecting point for later U.S. station modules and components.

The crew members of Space Shuttle STS-88 are as follows: Commander Bob Cabana, Pilot Fredrick Sturckow, Mission Specialist 1 Jerry Ross, Mission Specialist 2, Nancy Currie, Mission Specialist 3, James Newman, and Mission Specialist 4, Sergel Krikalev.

Commander Bob Cabana flew Endeavor to rendezvous with Zarya and Nancy Currie used the shuttles robotic arm to capture the Russian spacecraft and attach it to the Unity Node in the payload bay. At this time Zarya was the most massive object ever moved with the Remote Manipulator System (RMS).

Now it was time for the "Space Walkers" to hook up all of the umbilical connections and cables between the Utility Node and the Russian Spacecraft Zarya. Mission Specialist Jerry Ross and Jim Newman completed three space walks during the Shuttle STS-88 time in space. The two astronauts loving what they do best installed handrails, foot restraints sockets, early communications system antennas, and routing of the Communications cable from the Zarya to the starboard antenna. My team and I were in support of this mission, with Safety and Mission Assurance

This was the beginning of five more years of orbital assembly work that would construct the new Space Station.

EXPEDITION 1: STS-97, STS-98, AND STS-102 PLUS NATIONAL MANAGEMENT ASSOCIATION

Expedition 1 was the very first long-duration stay on the International Space Station (ISS). The three-person crew stayed aboard the station for 136 days from November 2000 to March 2001. It was the beginning of an uninterrupted human presence on the station, which has continued as of May 2020. Expedition 2, which also had three crew members, immediately following Expedition 1.

The official start of Expedition 1 began when the crew of 3 docked to the ISS on the second of November 2000, aboard the Russian spacecraft Soyuz TM-31, which had launched two days earlier. The Expedition 1 crew with one American, Bill Shephard Commander, and two Russians.

The Expedition 1 crew came prepared for a long stay in Space, this was all made possible by the Space Shuttles that came before, Like STS- 97, with a launch date of December I, 2000. The crew of STS-97 brought the first set of the solar arrays to the ISS, allowing the ISS to operate in space. The solar arrays were designed by Lockheed Corp. They had solar arrays mounted on a "Blanket", and this blanket could be folded like an accordion, to open up in space to a length of 112 feet by 39 foot wide.

For STS 97, two spacewalks were made to complete assembly operations of the first solar arrays, by Joe Tanner, Carlos Noriega, and Marc Garneau, all Mission Specialist. The solar arrays were mounted to a truss, the entire structure, a 17 ton package called the P6 Integrated Truss Segment. This will be the heaviest and largest element yet delivered to the ISS aboard a shuttle. The 50 ft. long Robotic Arm on the Shuttle will place the P3 integrated truss segment onto the ISS. All went as planned.

The crew of the STS-97: Tanner, Bloomfield, Gameau, Jett, and Noriega. The three Mission Specialist were busy installing the solar arrays, they also prepared a Docking port for the arrival of the Destiny Laboratory Module, and delivered supplies for the ISS Crew.

The second visiting Space Shuttle to the ISS was STS -98, launched on February 7, 2001 from Kennedy Space Center and docked to the ISS on February 9, 2001. With a crew of 5. Commander Kenneth D. Cockell, Pilot Mark L. Polansky, Mission Specialist 1, Robert L. Curbeam, Mission Specialist 2, Marsha S. Ivins, Mission Specialist 3, Thomas D. Jones

STS-98 delivered the Destiny Laboratory Module to the ISS. This Lab was built by the Boeing Corp. at the Michoud Facility in New Orleans La. (I remember working at this facility for the Saturn V Rocket Program, a long time ago.) All of the mission objectives were met. Again the crew of Expedition 1 welcomed the crew of the STS-98 to a welcome ceremony in the ISS. The Space Shuttle landed safely at Edwards Air Force Base on February 2001.

Space Shuttle STS-102 was the final Space Shuttle visit to Expedition 1. STS-102 came to exchange the Expedition 1 crew with the next three-person, long -duration crew for Expedition 2. This Shuttle was launched on March 8, 2001 from Kennedy Space Center and returned on March 21, 2001.

The other objective for this mission was to transfer a multi-purpose logistics module from the Shuttle cargo bay to the ISS.

The Crew for STS-102: Commander, James D Wetherbee, Pilot, James M. Kelly, Mission Specialist 1, Andrew W. Thomas, Mission Specialist2, Paul W. Richards. This Shuttle carried the long duration crew for the up-coming Expedition 2: with Vury V. Usachev, James S. Voss, and Susan J. Helms.

The returning flight with the crew for Expedition 1 went as planned, and the Crew were ever grateful to be going home. I provided Safety and Mission Assurance for all missions.

Space Shuttle STS-105 was the next Shuttle for crew rotation, other Shuttle's followed to bring supplies and do Spacewalks on the International Space Station.

The National Management Association (NMA) of the Lockheed Houston Chapter became a part of my life and, I joined as one who was interested in seeking a better leadership role in management for my life, my Faith, and my future.

I worked for a lot of Engineering Managers at NASA who had derived a lot of their management skills directly from this great association. So I joined this group of professionals. I remembered that leadership is a call to service, in fact this is a code of Ethics for this Association. There are 10 more code of Ethics all very important. The Founders of this Association stressed that "Benefits are Proportional to Involvement." This is very important, because each person who joins this Association must become active in their quest for excellence in Management.

All of my life I have been interested in leadership, and what it takes to become a good leader. As a leader, I must achieve serving the needs of my team.

My Manager was Mr. Brown, he would become my Mentor with his goal of helping me achieve my Leadership role in management. A mentor sees something in you that he can work with to help you become that leader of men and woman.

I had a long talk with my wife, who would become a big part of be joining this Association. The first thing I did was to sign up for NMA Classes that will help me learn to be a better leader in Management. This has helped me in so many ways as a Manager to build and lead groups to accomplish goals. I found myself working later in the evening because of the classes. When I did arrive home I was blessed to have an understanding wife to greet me.

I also began to volunteer my services to the National Management Association (NMA) in many ways. On way was to volunteer for the Company Picnic held once a year. Here is a good example of our Code of Ethics.

The NMA allowed me to stretch myself in ways I thought were impossible but nothing is impossible with **God.**

I was first assigned to the Professional Development Division at our company. My first job was to organize all of the seminars, and this included scheduling, Seminar announcement, and selection of Seminars. I choose to present a verity of Seminars, Financial, Tax, Free Enterprise, Wills, Trusts, and Estate Planning, Family Vacations on a Budget, and How to manage your retirement plan. By holding so many seminars, my Name was out there and it was respected by the National Management Association. This was service at its core.

I organized and lead a Total Quality Management Program (TQM) for my Company.

I was responsible for the organization and leading a Mentoring Program for all Lockheed employees. Later on, I helped **NASA** to have their own Mentoring Program. I was rewarded by **NASA** with a Certificate of Excellence.

The last thing I did while being employed was to organize and lead a team of Lockheed Employees for our first Lockheed Fitness Center. I still have the blue print that I drew for the Fitness Center, I will present it in my book.

I went on to finish all of my Management Classes, and this was no small task. My achievement of earning my _National Management Certification_ could not be possible without the help of my Faith, my fellow friends, my Mentor Mr. Brown and my dear Wife, always there by my side. I would not have accomplished all that I have without my **Lords** Support.

COLUMBIA'S LAST MISSION

Space Shuttle Columbia, STS -107, disintegrated over the State of Texas during re-entry on February 1, 2003. For this tragic event, we will trace the Space Shuttle movements and what was the primary reason for the death of all of the Astronauts on Board this Fateful day.

This Shuttle was launched from Kennedy Space Center on January 16, 2003, with a space Crew of seven Astronauts. <u>Commander</u> Rick D. Husband, USAF <u>Pilot</u>, William C. McCool, USN, <u>Mission Specialist 1,</u> David M. Brown USN, <u>Mission Specialist 2,</u> Kalpana Chawia , <u>Mission Specialist 3</u>, Michael P. Anderson, USAF, <u>Mission Specialist 4,</u> Laurel B. Clark USN, <u>Mission Specialist 5,</u> Ilan Ramon, Israeli Air Force.

The shuttle crew all agreed on their mission Insignia, it is the only Patch of the shuttle program that is entirely shaped in the orbiter's outline. The mission inclination is portrayed by the 39- degree angle of the Astronaut symbol to the Earth's horizon. The sunrise is representative of the numerous experiments that are the dawn of a new era for continued microgravity research on the International Space Station and beyond. The breadth of Science and the exploration of space is illustrated by the Earth and Stars. The constellation Columbia (the dove) was chosen to symbolize peace on Earth and the Space Shuttle Columbia.

The Seven Stars in the Mission Insignia also represent the <u>seven crew members</u> aboard this mission and also honor the <u>Original 7 Astronauts</u>

who paved the way to make research in space possible. Six stars have five points, the seventh star has six points like The Star of David, symbolizing the Israeli Space Agency's contributions to the Mission for Ilan Ramon. An Israeli flag is adjacent to the name of Payload Specialist Ramon, who was the first Israeli in space. Dr. Laurel Clark provided most of the design concepts for the patch.

As a research mission, this crew was kept busy 24 hours a day performing chores with science experiments. STS -107 carried the Spacehab Double Research Module, also the Freestar experiment and the Extended Duration Orbiter Pallet all in the Cargo Bay.

Onboard Columbia was a copy of a drawing by Petr Ginz, the Editor in—Chief of the Magazine Vedem, who drew what he imagined the Earth looked like from the moon, when he was a 14 year-old in the Terezin Concentration camp. This copy was in the possession of Ilan Ramon and was destroyed on the Shuttle reentry.

On returning to Earth over the state of Texas at about 9 AM Eastern time. The Space Shuttle Columbia began to break apart, the date was February 1, 2003.

A seven -month investigation followed, including a four- month search across Texas to recover debris. The search was head quartered at Barksdale Air Force Base in Sherport, LA. Almost 90 pieces of debris was shipped to Kennedy Space Center, and housed in the Columbia Debris Hanger. When the search for debris had ended, almost 38 percent of the Shuttle was recovered.

I am proud to have helped my oldest Son Bryan, who was chosen to search for debris. I will tread lightly when I tell you about finding human remains. Of course some remains of the Astronauts were also scattered across the Texas soil. The handling of the body parts was done by special trained government employees. The remains of the Astronauts will be handled with loving care and returned to their loved ones for final burial. This was a tragedy and a terrible loss to our Nation. This loss has been covered by many news outlets like the Houston Texas Chronicle, which I will use to help tell the story of this great tragedy along with my personal account.

The Shuttle was scheduled to arrive at its Kennedy Space Center landing strip at 8:16 a.m. The Space agency's oldest shuttle. Columbia was returning from it's 28th mission and represented 113th flight of a shuttle in the program's 22 year history.

The Shuttle debris was scattered all across Texas in Hemphill Texas, remains were found of an Astronaut, an intact charred helmet was found in San Augustine County, a V-shaped chunk of metal, was found in the median of U.S. 79 just northeast of Palestine, Texas, a –foot long metal bracket that had smashed through the roof of a dentist office in Nacogdoches Texas, a-2 foot square of metal was found in Cherokee County, Texas, the list goes on so much debris had fallen.

My Son Bryan and his team were able to tag special pieces of debris. During the debris recovery activities, some of the Columbia experiments were found. Scientists have indicated valuable science will still be produced. But most of the scientific data had been transmitted to the ground controllers and was saved.

The Clear Lake Community at **NASA** Johnson Space Center was in shock. This sense of loss was apparent throughout the community and the nation. People gathered to lay flowers and American flags at a makeshift memorial outside Johnson Space Center for each of the seven Astronauts. I remember this very well. This is a close- knit community with caring and respect for each person who works and lives out their lives at the Johnson Space Center. The seven lost astronauts were well known in this caring community. The chance of a tragedy happing is always there in our minds, and the people of this community thing about it every day.

For this is the price of <u>Exploration</u>, not one Astronaut thinks otherwise. Their life is geared towards Space, the un-known dangers does not keep them awake at night. Every Shuttle but one has brought the crew safely home. But on their return flight over Texas, the tremendous forces that assault a spacecraft during these few minutes of each mission found a <u>fatal flaw</u>. The Spacecraft was quick to break apart.

Those in the **NASA** Control Center began to voice their concerns as the Shuttle Columbia broke apart, this gave way to fear and concern for their fellow travelers. I have been in this Control Center many times, but this day will not be forgotten soon. Everyone their said a <u>prayer</u> for their friends.

Now let us focus on what was the root cause of the total disintegration of this Shuttle Mission.

Total Blame can be hard to come by, just what happened on this Mission? Immediately after the disaster, **NASA** convened the Columbia Accident Investigation Board to determine the cause of the disintegration. The Source of the failure was determined to have been caused by a large piece of ice and foam that had broken away during launch and had damaged the thermal protection tiles (reinforced carbon-panels). These panels are made by the Lockheed Corp. to keep the Shuttle free from the terrible blast of heat of re-entry. After this all Shuttle Missions would use the Remote Manipulator System with a camera attached to determine if any thermal panel tiles were damaged.

The damage to the thermal tiles on the shuttle left wing was similar to that on The Shuttle Atlantis had sustained back in 1988 during STS-27. However the damage on STS-27 occurred at a spot that had more robust metal and less tile damage, that mission survived the re-entry just fine.

So on re-entry of the shuttle, the lack of protection from the thermal protection tiles on the left wing of the shuttle caused it to overheat and this was the root cause of the break-up of Columbia. Another problem was the landing gear under the left wing to heat up and causing the tire to overinflate and explode thus adding more damage to the Shuttle.

The loss of Columbia prompts questions about NASA future. This was the second Shuttle disaster, this will stir fresh debate over the cost and justifications for space exploration at a time home land defense costs are soaring and an expensive war with Iraq is looming. For the Families of the fallen Astronauts, they expressed their grief and their sentiment that "we must find what went wrong and move on". For years critics have questioned the wisdom of spending $3 billion –a –year far the cost of the Shuttle Program. Until Shuttle flights resume the Russians assume responsible for the Space Station cargo and crew delivery requirements, but they have already warned the United States that financial problems could ground their capabilities.

A formal Memorial Service with over 10,000 attended was held at The Johnson Space Center for the seven Astronauts aboard Columbia but millions around our nation watched on television as President Bush consoled the families of the seven Astronauts and all of the NASA employees and the Contractors of NASA who worked with the Astronauts. Mourners who could not attend stood-side –by-side on the lawn off NASA RD. 1.

President Bush "The sorrow is lonely, but you are not alone" his address to all of the familys who lost loved ones, and those who were present at the memorial service Like myself and my family who was able to attend.

President Bush went on to say "For their mission was almost complete and we lost them so close to home." The men and women of the Columbia had journeyed more than 6 million miles and were minutes away from arrival and reunion."

President Bush assured the pubic that The Space Shuttle will continue in the future. "Bush said that this tragedy will not hinder Space Missions". "The cause in which they died will continue. Mankind is led into the darkness beyond our world by the inspiration of discovery and the longing to understand. Our journey into space will go on. In the Skies today, we saw destruction and tragedy, yet farther than we can see, there's comfort and hope. The same creator who names the stars also knows the names of the seven souls we mourn today. The crew of the shuttle Columbia did not return safely to Earth, yet we can pray that all are now safely home in Heaven". (I have a drawing of this crew going home to heaven, which I will place in my book). President Bush made his word come true, the Space Shuttle did continue flying after this tragedy in 2005 and ended all missions in 2011.

In his address to the Nation President Bush offered words from the Bible, from **Isaiah 40:26,** President Bush quoted from the <u>Prophet Isaiah</u> "Lift your eyes and look to the heavens. Who created all these? He who brings out the starry hosts one by one and calls them each by name. Because of his great power and mighty strength not one of them is missing."

From President Bush "May **God** bless the grieving families, and may **God** continue to bless America."

Now a reflection on Astronaut Ilan Ramon who also flew above his homeland, the land of Israel. "Ilan was a patriot; the devoted son of a Holocuaust survivor and had served his country in two wars. "Ilan, "said his wife Rona, "Left us at his peak moment in his favorite place, with people he loved".

The Men and Women of Columbia had journeyed more than 6 million miles and were coming home from the highest moments in their life, having achieved things most of us can't even fathom. I along with others, will grieve their loss and may our **Lord** welcome them safely into his home.

MY JOURNEYS END

After the Space Shuttle Columbia tragedy, I made the decision to retire from **NASA,** along with a lot of my fellow workers. There comes a time when retirement is the right thing to do. I received a good retirement package from my Company. I am blessed to have known and worked with so many wonderful friends at **NASA**. This has been a God blessed Odyssey of my Space and Faith Journey working with Space Shuttle Payloads and the Astronauts as Spacewalkers.

My voyage of Space and faith did not come easy. It was hard with all of the failures and setbacks that one must overcome. I reached my dreams by always believing in my Faith and staying the course thru hard times and good. And finally, see my dreams come true, by truly believing. One must believe in their self to overcome all fears one has to face. One also needs a plan to work towards becoming what you want in life. This means one plans for success, and if your plan is faith driven like mine, you must always follow where your faith compass leads you.

My dream of working for **NASA** began when I was blessed with having caring Mentors, who worked with me to make my dreams come true from High School thru College and beyond.

The **NASA** Space Program began with a dream of President John F. Kennedy in 1961 with a challenge to the people of the United States, to dream about putting a man on the moon and returning him safely back to earth. It was a challenge for each of us to look upward and dream.

Finally, we had President Kennedy, who was bold enough to match the Russians claim to Space with their new Satellite called Sputnik. We challenged the Russians, and the Space Race was on. President Kennedy said, "We must prove ourselves once again to the whole Nation." And with his passion for winning the space race with the Russians, we were victorious in the end.

During the end of **WW2,** we had a great President who acted in the **USA's** best interest to start the first Dream for all of mankind, a Rocket that would take Man to the Moon. In time this became The Saturn V Rocket.

Let us examine Wernher Von Braun, a German Rocket Scientist on the facts about his past history, working with the German Army in **WW2.** In Chapter two, I explained about my first job supporting **NASA** at the Saturn V Rocket Facility. Here I met Mr. Von Braun, I was young and eager to meet this great Scientist.

Operation **Paperclip,** was the secret American project to capture the German Scientist at the end of **WW2.** The USA must rescue the leading German Scientist at Nordhausen, an underground facility on the French Coast, before Russia could steal them. Here is a tale of daring and bravery, a plan was put into action, the US Army Rangers were sent to rescue the German Scientist, Wernher Von Braun and Dornberger, the masterminds behind the German V1 and V2 Rockets. Here the Germans used slave labor from Mittelbaun – Dora, a concentration camp. Here over 20,000 prisoners died at this location. A novel by James Mitchner, titled "Space" portrayed this story. Later on, a TV series of "Space" was made, and I was picked to play a minor part at the **NASA** Johnson Space Center. Both American and Soviet forces scrambled to capture the leading scientists. With information from French Resistance fighters, we were able to get a head start on the Russians. Werner Von Braun and Dornberger, plus other scientist were taken to the White Sands New Mexico Facility. Here with an actual V2 Rocket, tests were run. Later on, testing of the Redstone Rocket was started at **NASA** Huntsville Alabama. With this great rocket, we sent Astronauts into low Earth Orbit, during the Mercury Program and later on, for the Gemina Program. Later we built The Saturn V Rocket powerful enough to take man to the Moon. I was blessed to have helped design and work on this Great Rocket. Here I become friends with the most interesting people working on the Saturn V Rocket, like my good friend Rubin, a Russian Rocket Scientist.

As Hitler came to power, he supported the rearmament of the Army Rocket Program. Von Braun was totally sympathetic to the regime and moved upward in the Third Reich. What Von Braun did in this war for the sake of the German regime was wrong, no excuse can be found. After he was sent to White Sands, New Mexico to work on the V2 rocket, here he meet a man, who changed his life forever. Von Braun was converted, from a person who worshiped an idol, called Hitler, into a new man, who worshiped the true God.

After the tragedy of Space Shuttle Columbia, everything was completely shut down at NASA. My wife and I wanted to hang it up and just travel the World. The Space Shuttle tragedy put a different perspective on things. I began to think about life and how short it can be. There are so many things yet to accomplish. My wife, Susan, and I began to plan our next steps concerning travel, a more relaxed lifestyle, and work in the mission field. We have traveled a lot during my working days at **NASA,** mostly to Alaska and Colorado, doing a lot of exploring in the mountains. We were hikers, going the distance thru the Colorado Rockies, climbing upward to snowcapped mountains, there to experience peace and tranquility.

I have made The Woodlands, Texas home for a long time now. Susan and I have enjoyed our life here. My feet might stray to other places far away. But there are memories in this special place, to warm my soul and light my face, this dear place, is now is part of me.

My Father, a Navy Chief Petty Officer during WW2, came home from the South Pacific War when I was a very young boy. I asked my Dad if he thought I would ever be a success. He said sure, "if you were to walk from here to the mailbox your journey would be over. But remember Son, success is not a designation, it's a journey of life. "You will find success in many things along life's way so enjoy, all of your successes today and tomorrow". I have listened and acted on dad's words. My Father a wise and humble man, would tell everyone how proud he was of all my successes in life. I have learned what real success means, it is not about what I have achieved, but by the character, I have built in others. My Son Christopher, when he was a young lad, asked me, what have I accomplished in life? I remember what my dear old Father had said about success. I explained to my Son with love and pride that our **God** will let you have success in life, and when you do, give him all of the glory he is due.

My Space Odyssey has been a Space and Faith journey that has taken me into experiences that I never thought possible. I have so enjoyed my Journey as I was blessed by a loving **God.** By his providence, saw, that I was blessed beyond measure. I believe that our **Father** has a special purpose for everyone that believes in him, so much that I followed my Faith Compass, even when things were uncertain. I believe that I have accomplished many things working at **NASA** with my **Lord's** help. I have been good friends to all and numerous Astronauts, which I have helped each one on their (EVA) Spacewalks for Safety and Mission Assurance.

There are special people in my heart who left footprints. The ones who touched me in a way that I will not soon forget. A gentle word, some laughter we have shared. These footprints take me there. So when I'm missing all my friends–I'll reach softly towards my heart where footprints comfort me.

My space odyssey at **NASA** began in 1966, many years ago. In that time I have been blessed to have worked for one year on The **NASA** Saturn V Rocket Program in New Orleans La. After College I worked for **NASA,** Johnson Space Center in Clear Lake, Texas working for another 25 years. I have followed my dream; by supporting **NASA** in the field of Safety and Mission Assurance (S&MA) as an Engineer. It has allowed me to work with Apollo Moon Missions, Space Shuttle Missions, and the International Space Station. Working with Astronauts for their EVA Spacewalks and Mission Assurance. I was assigned to The Shuttle Avionics Integration Laboratory (**SAIL**) at Lyndon Johnson Space Center.

The Shuttle Avionics Integration Laboratory (**SAIL**) was the only facility in the Space Shuttle Program, where actual Space Shuttle hardware and flight software could be integrated and tested in a simulated flight environment. It supported the entire Space Shuttle Program to perform integrated verification tests. It also contained Firing Room Launch Equipment identical to that used at Kennedy Space Center. Thus complete ground verification as well as countdown and abort operations could be tested and simulated. I was blessed to have assisted so many Astronauts who chose to use the (**SAIL**) in preparing for their Space Shuttle Missions.

At the Shuttle Avionics Integration Laboratory, my Manager was Christopher Columbus Kraft Jr. This great man, earlier in life become the Flight Director at Johnson Space Control Center. Chris was flight director at some of the most iconic moments of Space History during the Mercury, Gemini, and Apollo Space Missions. He used his uncompromising management style which defined his control room operations and discipline. We stand on his shoulders, as we reach deeper into the solar system, and this man will always be with us on our space journeys.

I was assigned to the Department of Defense (DOD) of the Air Force for the Pacer Coin Project. The Pacer Coin Project is a reconnaissance and surveillance system, which provides imagery intelligence support in a C130E Hercules, and is operated and manned by the Lockheed USAF Services in California. The Pacer Coin Project later would be used to help support Peacekeeping Operations in the war in Bosnia.

I was also assigned to The Department of Defense (DOD) For Space Shuttle Missions, working with the Air Force. A lot of Space Shuttle Missions were classified as secret and some top secret.

I believe in being a servant in one's faith journey in life. I shared with you, the blessings of being a servant in several prior chapters. Our Shepard came to serve and to help the needs of others; so give me a servant's heart, **Lord,** Help me to reach out and share; Let them know I'm willing and let them see I care. Give me the courage to do your will each and every day; and fill me with your strength as I go along my way.

I was blessed to have been selected by my Company for the organization of a mentoring Program for all of our employees. This, I accepted with a humble heart.

I covered the Mentoring Program, "Foundations" in Chapter 10, I will now explain to you how this mentoring program has grown and what it means to me and countless employees of Lockheed Martin and **NASA.**

I have always appreciated each mentor in my life's journey from high school, through college, and beyond. One must mirror oneself thru other's vision, of what they see in you. We need mentors in our lives, a person who sees something of value or worth that you possess, but is hidden from you. A mentor can help you see your **God-** given value, to help you live out your life's journey.

A long time ago I was sent on a mission by my manager to lead a team for a new mentoring program. I searched, collected information for a mentoring program. I believed that if one does exist that meets our Company needs, one must always look to other leaders who have put a mentoring program in place for their Company. I found this Leader, a Miss Jeannie Kranz from Rockwell Corp. Jeannie and I became good friends and she was happy to help me. Jeannie named her new mentoring program "**Foundations-Building upon The Past.**"

This program was what our company was looking for, it contained everything to build a strong mentoring program for our employees. The title was perfect also, I stressed using "Foundations" for our Company and building on our past experience and accomplishments. My team and I put this great mentoring program in place for our company.

NASA at Johnson Space Center contacted Lockheed Martin about our Mentoring Program. They were interested in having a new mentoring program like ours put in place at **NASA**. My Manager selected me to interface with **NASA.** I was humbled, their management wanted a Mentoring Program like "Foundations" that would work for all of the **NASA** employees. After "Foundations" was installed and made available to the thousands of their employees, everyone was pleased with the outcome.

I believe with all of my heart our **God** can have more than one purpose for us in life. Without a doubt, one of his special purposes or blessings for me, was securing a Mentoring Program for Lockheed Martin and **NASA**. The benefits of mentoring are health, behavioral, relational, motivational, and career, to name a few of the great benefits. Over the years, the Mentoring Program, "Foundations", has made a lasting impact on the employees of Lockheed Martin and **NASA.** I have followed the success of this mentoring program over the years, and I am proud and blessed to have enabled over 80,000 employees of Lockheed Martin and **NASA** to benefit from this Mentoring Program of "Foundations." As the evening gates are closing, so my Space Odyssey must come to a close. There are Leaders who will come after me, and carry the torch once more. To lead our people, serve as they are needed, and continue to work for a higher cause, when they are called. And may they never stop their Space and Faith Journey in life.

Now it is time to prepare for our trip to see the land of Scotland, to experience Scotland's Legends and Lochs. Our journey will take us to Glasgow, Oban, Inverness, and Edinburg. MY wife and I have been looking forward to this trip for a very long time. My Great Grand Father, Henry Bell was from Scotland and here is my heritage. The Bell Clan first settled in the Scottish Highlands, but due to poor grazing land and extremely cold weather they later moved to the border region between Scotland and England. Here the land was good to raise crops, Scottish cows and sheep. The Bell Clan grew in number, I have a map showing this region where the Bell Clan have settled. (I will present this map in my book). The Bell Clan settled in Middlebie, Dumfriesshire and Berwickshire and in Edinburg Scotland. History was kind to the Bells, forging ahead in the invention of the Telephone, by Alexander Graham Bell, Born in Edinburg (1846- 1922). Mr. Henry Bell (1767-1830) designed the "Comet" the first steam powered ship. Sir Charles Bell (1774-1842) pioneered work on the human nervous system, and many more Bell's to build, invent, and make history.

We have come to Scotland to embrace the people, to explore the castles, and battlefields, and to experience the present and history of these brave people called Scotts. We will hike the Highlands of the Glen Nevis at Glencoe and on Ben Nevis the highest mountain in Scotland. Heading from Glencoe we will arrive in Inverness to experience the capital of the Highlands. Here we will go by ferry to the Isles of Skye. While in Inverness we will stay in a B&B, ready to explore the area for the last great battle of free loving Scotts, the battle of Culloden Moor. On this battlefield around 2,000 Scottish Jacobites of this great army were killed by a British force on the 16th of April, 1746. A lone Scottish piper can be heard, as the sweet music of freedom echoing in the Highlands once more. The uprising of the Scottish Jacobites was for freedom from the British rule. Much later they gained their freedom, a separate free Scotland with Scottish laws.

We have enjoyed our stay in Scotland, meeting so many wonderful Scotts, loving every minute on our hikes in the mountains and always embracing life. We will listen to stories from our past, stories our ancestors have handed down to us. We have traveled many a mile, seeing the Highlands and now to visit what they call the Lowlands of Scotland. Go with us on this exciting Journey as we explore this area of Scotland.

Lord I want to travel the Higher Road with you, to walk the path that you are on. I don't need to see the switchbacks on this trail, with you Lord, all fears are gone. There are always troubled spots in every trail, just as there is sunshine following rain. And if I should stumble on a rocky ledge, your strong outstretched hand will lift me up again. Yes I want to walk the Higher Road that all good Scotts must take. Please help comfort me on my journey, for we cannot see the pitfalls that lie ahead, but, we know the One who's guiding to the glories at its end.

Lightning Source UK Ltd.
Milton Keynes UK
UKHW020001111022
410275UK00013B/74/J